Qadianism

A Critical Study

Syed Abul Hasan Ali Nadwi

Translated from the Urdu by
Zafar Ishaq Ansari

NADWI PRESS

NADWI PRESS

Nadwi Press Edition

Find our titles on your favourite online bookstore using the keyword 'Nadwi Press'

Originally Published by AIRP, Lucknow (India)
Reprinted by Nadwi Press in 2025

Translation of the Qur'ān

It should be perfectly clear that the Qur'ān is only authentic in its original language, Arabic. Since perfect translation of the Qur'ān is impossible, we have used the translation of the meaning of the Qur'ān throughout the book, as the result is only a crude meaning of the Arabic text.

Qur'ānic verses appear in speech marks proceeded by a reference to the Surah and verse number. Sayings (Hadith) of Prophet Muhammad (saw) appear in inverted commas along with reference to the Hadith Book and its Reporter.

Contents

Preface

In the name of Allah, the Benevolent, the Merciful

Towards the end of December 1957, and in the beginning of January 1958, an International Islamic Colloquium was held in Lahore under the auspices of the Punjab University in which a large number of distinguished and noted scholars of the Muslim world and Western countries took part. Quite a few outstanding ulama representing Middle Eastern countries were there. Despite having received an invitation to participate the writer was unable to reach Lahore until after the colloquium had ended. The points that had been raised during the colloquium continued to be debated by many people.

The scholars who had come from Egypt, Syria and Iraq to participate in the conference showed considerable keenness to collect correct information about the fundamental beliefs and doctrines of Qadianism, the well-known religious movement of India and Pakistan. This curiosity on their part was justified and natural. For, it was in this part of the world that Qādiānism was born and developed. Hence, from here alone authentic material and information could be procured. The Pakistani and Indian friends of these guests felt the existence of a serious lacuna: the absence of any book on the subject in present-day Arabic which could be presented to them. It was owing to this feeling that when the writer reached Lahore he was ordered by his spiritual teacher and guide, Hazrat Maulānā 'Abdul Qadir Raipurī, to write a book on this subject in Arabic.

During his trips to the Middle East and his stay in Egypt and Syria the writer had himself felt the need of such a work, but the subject had failed to capture his imagination. The subject was on the whole, out of tune with his temperament. Despite his repeated efforts, the writer did not succeed in forcing himself to study any of Mirza Ghulām Ahmad's writings. Hence, when he undertook the task, he had little familiarity with the subject. But the demand had been made from a personage the compliance of whose wish was a matter of deepest spiritual satisfaction, to the writer, and this enabled him to devote himself to a thorough study of Qādiānism. Within a few days, the room where the writer was staying at Lahore changed into a full-fledged library on Qadianism. The work then started in earnest, and for one month the writer remained so deeply immersed in the subject that he lost almost all touch with the outside world and had his mind free for no other subject.

The writer's mental framework being that of a student of history, he launched upon his intellectual journey from the very beginning of the movement, surveying every stage in its progress and development. The writer's observations, therefore, moved along the lines through which Qadianism had passed during its course of development. This approach helped the writer to grasp the real nature of the Qädiāni movement, its gradual evolution, and its motivating factors. This approach uncovered a number of aspects which might have remained hidden otherwise. The writer delved deep into the writings of the founder of this movement, Mirza Ghulam Ahmad Qadiani, and it is through this first-hand source that he has tried to arrive at unprejudiced conclusions, trying to maintain the detachment of a historian in respect of the message, the movement, and the practical achievements of Qadianism. The result of this study has been published in the form of al-Qadiyani wa al-Qādiyānīyah in Arabic.

After the book had been prepared, Hazrat Maulāna 'Abdul Qadir ordered its translation into Urdu. Since actual excerpts in

Urdu were required for the Urdu edition, an entire library of books available only in Lahore was required once again. Another trip was made, after which this book was rendered into Urdu. This Urdu edition could better be regarded as an independent work because a number of valuable additions and modifications have been made during the process of it preparation.

For some time, literature on controversial religious subjects has had a peculiar language and style, so much so that this language and style have come to be regarded as part and parcel of religious writings. This writer has not considered himself bound by this polemical tradition. This book has been written with historical objectivity rather than the bigoted zeal of a debater. This will perhaps disappoint those who have been used to polemical writings. For this the writer offers no apology. The class of people for whom it has been written and the purpose which actuated its writing did not warrant any other style of expression.

The writer thanks all those friends and well-wishers who have been a source of guidance in the study of the subject, who provided him with the material needed for writing this book, and for facilitating the completion of the work. If this book serves Islam in any way, all such people share its reward.

The writer wishes to impress on his readers one thing: wisdom requires that a person should refrain from risking even as trivial a thing as one's monetary savings, and one should be careful in choosing the people to whom these should be entrusted. If wisdom demands such precaution in worldly affairs, it should not be difficult to guess what a tremendous amount of precaution should be exercised in the matter of faith on which depends a person's salvation and his felicity in the eternal life of the Hereafter. It is evident that in such a matter one should exercise extreme precaution; one should try to use one's discretion to the utmost, and to divest oneself of all emotional predilections, worldly attachments, and material interests. This book, through its authentic and systematically arranged information obtained from the statements and writings of the founder of Qadianism himself and through authentic historical information about the movement, can prove of help to many a person to arrive at an intelligent appreciation of Qâdiānism.

11, Rabi al- Awwal, 1378 S. Abul Hasan Ali Nadwi

PART I:
The Historical Background of the Rise of Qadianism

1: Muslim India in the Nineteenth Century

The nineteenth century is a period of unique importance in modern history. It is the century in which intellectual unrest and various kinds of conflicts and tensions found in the Muslim world reached their climax. India was one of the main centres of this unrest and tension. Here the conflicts and tensions between the Western and the Eastern cultures, between the old and the new systems of education, in fact, between the old and the new worldviews, and between Islam and Christianity were mounting. The forces concerned were locked in a fierce struggle for survival.

The movement began at a time when the well-known struggle of 1857 for the country's independence had been suppressed. This had shocked the Muslims to the core; their hearts were bleeding, and their minds paralysed. They were confronted with the danger of double enslavement; political as well as cultural. On the one hand, the victorious power, the British, had launched upon a vigorous campaign to spread a new culture and civilization in India. On the other hand, the Christian missionaries were scattered all over India bent upon active proselytization. To be able to shake the confidence of Muslims in their own beliefs and to make them skeptical as to the bases of the Islamic Shariah, even though they might not be converted to Christianity, was deemed by them an important enough achievement. The new generations of Muslims, which had not been thoroughly grounded in Islam, were their main target. The schools and colleges which were introduced along the foreign pattern were the main fields of their activity directed at spreading intellectual confusion. The efforts were not altogether unsuccessful and even incidents of conversion to Christianity began to take place in India. But the main danger of that period was not apostasy (in the sense of ostensible con- version from Islam to Christianity), but skepticism and atheism. Religious debates between Muslim ulama and Christian missionaries took place frequently, leading in general to the victory of the 'ulama of Islam. This established the intellectual superiority and greater vitality of Islam as against Christianity. Nevertheless, intellectual unrest, skepticism, and weakness of faith grew apace.

This was one aspect of the situation: the situation vis-à-vis the external menace. Looked at internally, the situation was even worse. Mutual disagreements between Muslim sects had assumed frightful proportions. Each sect was busy denouncing the other. Sectarian polemics were the order of the day, leading often to violent clashes, even to bloodshed, to litigation over controversial sectarian issues. The whole of India was in the grip of what might be termed a sectarian civil war. This too had given birth to mental confusion and created breaches in the Muslim society and disgust in the people and had considerably damaged the prestige of the Muslim ulama and of Islam.

On the other hand, immature süfis and ignorant pretenders of spiritual excellence had reduced the Sufi orders to a play- thing. They gave wide publicity to their trance-utterances and inspired pronouncements. One found people everywhere making overly extravagant claims and going about proclaiming their ability to perform astounding miracles and to receive messages from on High. The result of all this was that the Muslim masses had developed an uncommon relish for things esoteric, for miracles, for supernatural performances, for inspired dreams and prophesies. The more a person had to offer people by way of these things, the greater was his popularity. Such people used to become the centre of popular veneration. Hypocritical *darvishes* and cunning traders of religion took full advantage of the situation. People had developed such a liking for esoterics that they were readily prepared to accept every new fantasy, to support every new movement and to believe in every esoteric claim however baseless and imaginary. Muslims were generally in the grip of frustration and had fallen prey to defeatism. The failure of the struggle of 1857 and of a number of other recent religious and militant movements was fresh in their memory. Many of them had despaired, therefore, of bringing about any change and reform through normal processes and a large number of people had begun to await the advent of some charismatic personality, some divinely appointed leader. At places one heard that at the turn of the century the Promised Messiah would make his appearance. In religious gatherings people commonly referred to the numerous forms of misguidance and evil which were to appear on the eve of the Doomsday. Prophesies and esoteric statements such as those of Shah Niamat Ullah Kashmiri helped people to forget the bitterness of the current situation and strengthened their morale. Dreams, prophesies and other esoteric pronouncements had magnetic appeal and kept their spirits high.

The province of Punjab, in particular, was the centre of mental confusion and unrest, superstitions and religious ignorance. This province had suffered for eighty years under the yoke of the Sikh Raj, an overbearing military tyranny. During this period the religious belief and devotion of Muslims had weakened considerably. True Islamic education had been almost non-existent for long. The foundations of Islamic life and Islamic society had been shaken. Their minds were seriously in the grip of confusion and perplexity. In brief, to borrow the words of Iqbal:

The Khälsa (Sikhs) took away both the Qur'an and the sword,
In their realm, Islam was just dead.

This situation had paved the ground in the Punjab for the rise of a new religious movement based on novel interpretations and esoteric doctrines. The temperament of a good number of people of the region where this movement arose has been portrayed by Iqbal in these words:

In religion, he is fond of the latest,
He stays not for long at a place; he keeps on moving;
In learning and research, he does not participate,
But to the game of Mentors and Disciples, he readily succumbs;
If the trap of explanation anyone lays,
He walks into it quickly from the branch of his nest.

It was towards the end of the nineteenth century that Mirzā Ghulam Ahmad appeared on the scene with his unique message and movement. For the spread of his message and for the fulfilment of his ambitions Mirza Ghulam Ahmad found a fertile ground and a congenial period of time. He had numerous factors to his advantage-the general unrest in the minds of people, the exotic-loving temperament of the people, the general despair with regard to the efficacy of moderate and normal means of reform and revolution, the decline in the prestige of and confidence in the 'ulama, the popularity of religious debates which had vulgarised the religious curiosities and propensities of the people and made them, to a large extent, free- thinkers. Furthermore, the British rulers (who had had a bitter experience with Mujahidin movement and felt, therefore, considerable consternation for the spirit of jihad and the religious enthusiasm of Muslims), warmly welcomed this new religious movement which pledged loyalty to the British government and even made this loyalty an article of faith, and whose founder had had a long and close association with the government. All these factors provided the congenial atmosphere in which Qadianism came into existence, won converts, and developed into an independent sect and religion.

Mirza Ghulam Ahmad Qadiani[1]

Family Background

Genealogically Mirza Ghulam Ahmad belonged to the Barlās branch of the Moghuls[2]. But after some time, he came to know by means of 'inspiration' that he was, in fact, of Persian origin. To quote his own words:

"The revelation (*ilham*) about me is that: Were it that faith was hanging from the Pleiades it would still have been seized by the man from Persia[3]. And then, there is also a third revelation about me: Verily, those who disbelieved the man from Persia disproved their religions. God is thankful for his endeavour. All these 'revelations' show that our forefathers were Persian. And the truth is what Allah has made manifest."[4]

In one of his works, he writes:

"It should be remembered that apparently the family of this humble one is that of the Moghuls. No record has been

---

[1] This chapter purporting to lay down the biographical outlines of the founder's life is based chiefly on the statements and writings of the Mirzā himself, supplemented by the work of his son Mirzā Bashir Ahmed, Sirat al-Mahdi and other standard works of the Qadianis.

[2] Mirza Ghulam Ahmad, Kitāb al- Bariyah, p. 134 p.

[3] This tradition occurs in the Sihah with a little variation of words. In some reports there occurs the phrase 'Rijal Min Faras' (men from Persia) instead of Rajul (a man). The ulama and the muhaddithin interpret this hadith to refer to Salman al-Färisi and other ulama and holy men of Persia famous for their devotion and service to the cause of faith including the Imam Abu Hanifa, who was also of Persian origin.

[4] *Kitab al- Bariyah*, p. 135 n.

seen in the history of our family, showing that the family was Persian. What has been seen in certain records is that some of our grandmothers were of noble and noted Sayyid families. Now it has come to be known through the word of God that ours is a Persian family. We believe in this with all our conviction since the reality in respect of genealogies is known to none the way it is known to Allah, the Exalted. It is His knowledge alone which is true and sure and that of all others, doubtful and conjectural."[5]

Mirzā Gul Mohammad, the great grandfather of Mirzā Ghulam Ahmad owned considerable property. In Punjab he had a good-sized estate. Mirzā Ghulam Ahmad had mentioned in detail the aristocratic pomp and splendour of this ancestor of his, his habit to feed a large number of people at his table, and his religious influence.[6]

After his death, his estate declined, and the Sikhs confiscated the villages of that estate. This decline continued to such an extent that no other land remained in the ownership of his grandfather, Mirzā 'Atā Mohammad, except Qādian. Later on, the Sikhs occupied even that and drove the Mirzā family out of Qadian. During the last years of Ranjit Singh's rule Mirzā Ghulam Murtaza, the father of the Mirzā, returned to Qadian and the Mirzā later received five villages out of the landed property of his father.[7]

The Mirza's family maintained very loyal and cordial relations with the recently established British power in the Punjab. Several members of the family had shown great enthusiasm in

---

[5] Araba'in, Vol. II, p. 17 n.

[6] Kitab al- Bariyah, pp. 136-42 n.

[7] Ibid, pp. 142-44 n.

consolidating the new government and had come to its rescue on several critical occasions. To cite the words of the Mirzā himself:

> "I come from a family which is out and out loyal to this government. My father, Murtaza, who was considered its well-wisher, used to be granted a chair in the Governor's Durbar and has been mentioned by Mr. Griffin in his History of the Princes of Punjab. In 1857 he helped the British Government beyond his power, that is, he procured cavaliers and horses right during the time of Mutiny. He was considered by the Government to be its loyal supporter and well-wisher. A number of testimonials of appreciation received by him from the officers have unfortunately been lost. Copies of three of them, however, which had been published a long time ago, are reproduced on the margin. Then, after the death of my grandfather, my elder brother Mirza Ghulam Qadir continually occupied himself with service to the Government and when the evildoers encountered the forces of the British Government on the highway of Tammun, he participated in the battle on the side of the British Government."[8]

Birth, Education, Upbringing

The Mirzā was born during the last phase of the Sikh rule in the year 1839 or 1840 at Qadiān in Gurdaspūr District.[9] His own

---

[8] Ishtihar Wajib al- Izhār, September 20, 1897 pp. 3-6 appended with Kitab al-Bariyah.

[9] Kitāb al-Bariyah, p. 146, n. Mirza Bashiruddin Mahmood in his Address to the British Crown Prince in 1922, has mentioned the year of his birth to be 1837 (p. 35). According to this, in 1857, his age would be 21. This alteration seems to have been made in order to vindicate the Mirza's prophecy which has been mentioned

writings show that at the time of the struggle of Independence in 1857, he was sixteen or seventeen years old.[10]

The Mirzā received his education up to the Middle Class at home. He studied books on Grammar, Logic and Philosophy under the guidance of Maulavi Fazl-i-Ilahi, Maulavi Fazl-i-Ahmad and Maulavi Gul 'Ali Shah. He studied Medicine from his father who was an experienced physician. During his student life, the Mirzā was very studious. To quote his own words:

"During those days I was so thoroughly engrossed in books as if I was not present in the world. My father used to instruct me repeatedly to curtail my reading, for, out of sympathy for me he feared that this might affect my health." This, however, did not continue for long. Under the insistent pressure of his father, the Mirzā had to engage himself in the endeavour to get back his ancestral landed property which subsequently led to litigation in law courts. He writes:

"I feel sorry that a lot of my valuable time was spent in these squabbles and at the same time my respected father made me supervise the affair of landlord ship. I was not a man of this nature and temperament."[11]

---

by him as a Divine inspiration in the following words: "We shall cause you to live a good life for eighty years or close to that" (vide Araba'in, Vol. III, p. 39).

[10] Kitāb al-Bariyah, p. 146, n. Mirza Bashiruddin Mahmood in his Address to the British Crown Prince in 1922, has mentioned the year of his birth to be 1837 (p. 35). According to this, in 1857, his age would be 21. This alteration seems to have been made in order to vindicate the Mirza's prophecy which has been mentioned by him as a Divine inspiration in the following words: "We shall cause you to live a good life for eighty years or close to that" (vide Araba'in, Vol. III, p. 39).

[11] Kitab al- Bariyah p. 151.

The Mirzā later took employment with the Deputy Commissioner of Sialkot for a small salary. He remained for four years in this service, that is, from 1864 to 1868.[12] During this period he also read one or two books of English.[13] Moreover, he also took the examination of Mukhtar but flopped.[14] In 1868 he resigned this job and came to Qadian and began to look after his landed property. But most of his time was spent on reflecting on the Holy Qur'an and studying works of Tafsir and Traditions.[15]

Moral Disposition

From his very childhood, the Mirzā was very simple. He was unaware of worldly matters and appeared to be a little absent-minded. He did not even know how to wind a watch.[16] When he had to know time, he took out the watch from his pocket and began to count, starting from one. And even then, while he counted with his finger, he also kept on counting the figures aloud lest he should forget."[17] He could not just look at the watch and find out what time it was. Due to absent-mindedness, it was difficult for him to differentiate between the shoes of the left and the right feet. Mirzā Bashir Ahmad writes:

"Once someone brought for him *gurgabi* (a kind of shoes used in Punjab). He put them on but could not

---

[12] Sirat al- Mahdi, Vol. I., p. 44.

[13] Ibid. p. 155.

[14] Ibid p. 156

[15] Kitab al- Bariyah, p. 155 n.

[16] Qazi Mohammad Zuhūruddin Qādiyāni's article, Yad- i- Ayyam- Journal al-Hakam, May 21, 1934

[17] Sirat al- Mahdi, Vol. I, p. 180.

distinguish between the right and the left. Often, he used to wear them on the wrong feet, and then feel uncomfortable. Sometimes when he would be hurt by the use of the wrong shoe, he would get irritated and say that nothing of those people was good. Mother said that she had inscribed signs indicating right and left on the shoes for the sake of his convenience and yet he used to put the shoes on the wrong feet. Hence, she later removed the signs."[18]

Due to very frequent micturition the Mirza used to keep earthen-marbles[19] in his pockets. He also carried lumps of *gur*[20] for he was excessively fond of sweets.[21]

Mirza's Physical Health

In his youth, the Mirzā was so afflicted with hysteria that sometimes he used to fall down unconscious as a result of hysteric fits.[22] The Mirzā used to interpret these fits variously as hysteric and melancholia. He also suffered from diabetes and copious urination. Mentioning at one place that 'I am a permanently sick person,' he adds:

"Headache and giddiness and insomnia and palpitation of the heart come by fits, and the lingering ailment in the lower part of my body is that of diabetes. Often, I urinate up to a hundred times during the day or night. And all the other

---

[18] Sirat al- Mahdi, Vol. I. p. 67.

[19] Used after urination by Muslims for cleaning purposes, usually, when water is not available.

[20] An unrefined kind of sugar used in India.

[21] Burahīn- i- Ahmadiyah, Vol. I, p. 67.

[22] Sirat al- Mahdi, Vol, I, p. 17.

disorders of debility and exhaustion which are the natural results of such excessive urination have also fallen to my lot."[23]

In his youth, the Mirzā engaged himself in vigorous spiritual exercises and courses of rigid self-discipline. He also fasted continuously for long periods of time. In one of his long spells of spiritual exertion, he fasted continuously for six months.[24] In 1886, he passed another period of exclusive worship and prayer at Hoshiarpur.[25] Later on, due to ill health and debility, he had to give these up. On March 31, 1891, he wrote to Nūruddin: "Now my health can no longer bear the rigours of supererogatory devotion and even a little bit of severe devotion and meditation or contemplation causes illness."[26]

Economic Condition

The Mirzā began his life in ordinary circumstances: a life of hardship and poverty. But as his mission spread and he became the spiritual head of a prosperous sect, he grew prosperous and began to lead a comfortable life. He, too, was conscious of this change in his state: the ostensible difference between his earlier and later periods of life. In 1907, he wrote:

"Our living and our well-being had depended solely on the meagre income of our father. Among outsiders, none knew me. I was an unknown person, living in the desolate village of Qadian, lying in a corner of anonymity. Then, God, according to His prophecy, turned

---

[23] Appendix to Arba'in, p. 3/4 and p. 4 (abbreviated).

[24] Sirat al- Mahdi, Vol. I, p. 76.

[25] Ibid., p. 71.

[26] Makūbät- i- Ahmadiyah, Vol. V, No. 2, p. 103.

a whole world towards me and helped us by such continuous victories that I have no words to express my thanks. Considering my own position, I did not hope to receive even ten rupees a month. But the Exalted Allah, who raises the poor from dust and brings the arrogant down to the earth, helped me to such an extent that until now I have received about three hundred thousand rupees or, may be, even more."[27]

In the footnote, he adds:

"Although thousands of rupees have come by means of money orders, yet more have been passed on to me directly by sincere friends as gifts, or in the shape of currency notes enclosed with letters. Some sincere people have sent currency notes or gold anonymously and I do not even know what their names are."[28]

Marriage and Children

The Mirza's first marriage took place in 1852 or 1853 with one of his own relatives.[29] This wife gave birth to two sons: Mirzā Sultan Ahmad and Mirza Fazal Ahmad. In 1891, he divorced the lady. In 1884 he took another wife, the daughter of Nawab Nasir of Delhi.[30] The rest of the offsprings of the Mirzā were all from this wife. Three sons were born from her: Mirzā Bashiruddin Mahmood, Mirzā Bashir Ahmad (author of Sirat al-Mahdi) and Mirzā Sharif Ahmad.

---

[27] Haqiqat al- Wahy, p. 211.

[28] Ibid., p. 211, no.

[29] Sirat al- Mehdi, Vol. II, p. 150.

[30] Sirat al- Mahdi, Vol. II, p. 151.

Death

When in 1891 the Mirzā declared that he was the Promised Messiah[31], and later on in 1910, that he was a prophet of God,[32] the Muslim ulama began to refute and oppose him. Among those prominent in opposing him was Maulana Sanaullah Amritsari, the editor of Ahl-i-Hadith. On April 5, 1907, Mirzā Ghulam Ahmad issued an announcement in which, while addressing the said Maulana, he wrote:

> "If I am such a big liar and impostor as you portray me in each issue of your magazine, then I will die in your lifetime, for I know that the life-period of a mischief-maker and liar is not very long and ultimately he dies an unsuccessful man, during the life of his greatest enemies and in a state of humiliation and grief. And if I am not a liar and impostor and have been honoured by God's communication and address to me, and if I am the Promised Messiah, then I hope that with the grace of God and in accordance with God's practice you will not escape the punishment of the rejectors (of Truth). Thus, if that punishment which is not in man's but in God's hand, that is, fatal diseases like plague and cholera, do not afflict you during my lifetime,[33] then I am not from God."[34]

One year after the publication of this announcement, on May 25, 1908, the Mirzā fell ill, being afflicted with diarrhoea at Lahore. Along with loose motions, he also had vomiting. He was put under

---

[31] Refer Part II, Chapter 2.

[32] Refer Part II, Chapter 3.

[33] It would be interesting to note that Maulānā Amritsari died at the age of eighty on March 18, 1948, some forty years after the death of the Mirzā.

[34] Tabligh- i- Risalat, Vol. 120.

treatment at once, but weakness increased, and his condition became critical. The next day, on May 26, he breathed his last in the forenoon. About his death his father- in-law Mir Nāsir Nawab has stated:

> "The night on which Hazrat Mirzā Sahib fell ill, I was asleep at my place. When he felt very uncomfortable, I was awakened. When I went to Hazrat Sahib, he addressed me and said, 'Mir Sahib, I am ill with cholera'. After this, in my opinion, he did not speak a clear word till he died the next day after ten o'clock."[35]

The dead body was carried to Qādian. On May 27, 1908, the burial took place, and Hakim Nūruddin became his successor, the first Khalifah of the Qadiani movement.

[35] Hayat- i- Nasir, ed. Shaykh Yaqub Ali Irfani.

The Qadiani Saint Paul

Hakim Nüruddin Bhairawi occupies a position of unique importance in the history of Qadianism, second only to that of its founder. In fact, some observers are of the view that the said Hakim was the real brain behind the movement, that the intellectual currents of this movement sprang from his mind.

Birth and Early Education

Hakim[36] Nūruddin was born in 1258 A.H. (1841 A. D.) in Bhaira, District Sargodha (Punjab).[37] Thus, in 1857 he was 16 years of age and was younger than the Mirzā by just one or two years. His father, Hafiz Ghulam Rasul, was an imam in a mosque in Bhaira, and was a Farūqi by lineage.

The Hakim's early education took place in his home-village. He read the books on Fiqah in Punjabi language under the guidance of his mother. Then he went to Lahore. He was taught Persian by Munshi Qāsim Kashmir! and learnt calligraphy from Mirzā Imām Dayrawi. But neither of the two attracted him. Both his teachers were Shias. In 1272 A. H. (1855 A. D.) he returned home and remained for some time studying under Miän Häji Sharfuddin. It is around this time that he began to learn. the Arabic language systematically.

---

[36] Hakim means a physician practising the traditional system of Greek- Arabian medicine (Translator).

[37] These are based on Akbar Shah Khan Najibābādi's Mirgāt al-Yaqin fi Hayat Nüruddin. Najibābādi was a pupil of the Hakim. These biographical details were related to him by the Hakim himself at the time when Najibabadi was his student as well as a devout follower.

Under the influence of a bookseller who belonged to the movement of Sayyid Ahmad Shahid, there. arose in him the urge to translate the Holy Qur'an, and he anxiously read Taqwiyatul Iman and Mashariq-al-Anwar. A little later, he returned to Lahore and acquired some knowledge of Medicine. While his education was at a very advanced stage, he took employment with the Normal School, Rawalpindi. There he taught Persian and at the same time learned Arithmetic and Geography from another teacher. After passing a tahsil examination, he became headmaster in Pindi Dandan Khan and once more resumed the study of Arabic. After four years, he ceased to remain in service and began to devote all his time to his own studies. For some time, he studied under Maulavi Ahmaduddin (who was known as Buggiwāle Qāzī Sāhib). Then, his love for knowledge made him travel to several parts of India. In Rampur he resumed his studies: studied Mishkat-al-Masabih under Maulānā Hasan Shah, Sharah-i-Wigāyah under Maulavi Azizullah Afghānı, Usul of al-Shashi and Maibāzi under Maulānā Irshad Husain; the Diwan of al-Mutanabbı under Maulavī Sa'dullah; Sadra, etc., under Maulavı 'Abd al-'Alī, and the higher books on Logic like Mar Zahid Risalah and Mir Zahid Mulla Jalal, half-heartedly. At this time, he enthusiastically supported Ismail Shahid and sometimes used to speak to his teachers with great boldness. From Rampur he went to Lucknow and began to study medicine under a famous physician, Hakim Ali Husain. When 'Alī Husain went to Rampur on invitation from Nawab Kalb-i-Ali Khān of Rampur Nūruddin accompanied him. During his stay in Rampur, he further studied literature under Mufti Sa'dullah. On the whole he remained with Hakim Ali Husain for a period of two years and then went to Bhopal in order to complete his education in Arabic and to study Hadith. Bhopal, in those days, had become a great centre of learning. The Governmental patronage of knowledge and learning had attracted a good number of scholars.

In Bhopal he stayed with and was patronised by Munshi Jamaluddin Khan, the Chief Minister. During his stay, Nüruddin took lessons in Bukhari and Hidayah from Maulānā 'Abdul Qayyūm (the son of Maulana Abdul Hai Burhanwai, who was a Khalifah of Hazrat Sayyid Ahmad Shahid). From Bhopal he went on a visit to the Holy cities-Mecca and Medina-in order to complete his education and also in order to attain other-worldly felicity.[38]

In Mecca, he studied Abu Daud under Shaykh Muhammad Khazraji, Sahih Muslim under Sayyid Husain and began to study *Musallam al-Thubut under Maulānā Rahmatullah Kayrānawi*, the author of Izhar al-Haqq. Sometimes, he had heated discussion with his teachers and showed trends towards non- conformity and exaggerated confidence in the soundness of his own views and intelligence.[39]

At Mecca he finished his study of Abu Daüd and Ibn Majah under Shaykh Muhammad Khazraji. In the meantime, Shah 'Abdul Ghani Mujaddidi had arrived in Mecca. Later on, when Shah Mujaddidi returned to Medina, the Hakim joined him and, after taking an oath of allegiance to him remained as his student for six months.

---

[38] An interesting anecdote is related in this connection, which was narrated by Nūruddin himself. While leaving for the Holy cities, he asked Maulana Abdul Qayyüm to tender him some advice. He said, "Never become God or Prophet." "Abdul Qayytüm explained that by 'not becoming God' what he had meant was that if any of his desires were frustrated, he should not feel greatly dejected, for to be able to do what one likes is the attribute of God alone; by 'not becoming the Prophet' he meant that if people rejected his fatwas, he should not deem them to be condemned to hell, for it is the disobedience of the Prophet alone which condemns one to hell (*Mirgāt al-Taqin*, p. 79).

[39] *Miqāt al- Taqin* p. 95-97.

Occupation

After pilgrimage and visit to the Holy places, Nūruddin returned to his native place, Bhaira and stayed there for some time. During his stay he debated with people as to whether the current customs and usages conformed to the teachings embodied in the collections of Hadith which turned some people against him. This led him to realise the ignorance and stagnation of the common people and his own superiority and intellectual excellence. He also went to Delhi during the Durbar of Lord Lytton and there met Munshi Jamaluddin Khan, the Chief Minister of Bhopal, who brought him to Bhopal. After a short stay at Bhopal, Nūruddin once more went back to Bhaira and started practising medicine there. Soon his reputation as a successful physician spread and he was invited by the Mahārāja of Jammu to serve him as his personal physician. For a considerable period of time, he served the ruler of Jammu, Poonch and Kashmir and gained considerable influence there by dint of his ability as a physician, and his eloquence, knowledge and wit. He had become a very close confidant of the Mahārāja and thus quite powerful.

An Ardent Follower of Mirza

There were many similarities of character and temperament between Hakim Nūruddin and Mirza Ghulam Ahmad. It is difficult to say how they came into contact with each other. Their first meeting, however, took place at Qadian in 1885. When the Mirzā wrote *Barahin-i-Ahmadiya*, Nūruddin wrote a book supporting it. His admiration for the Mirza increased so much so that he took an oath of allegiance at his hands and accepted him as his spiritual guide, his leader, and pledged to follow him. The following letter of Nūruddin shows the depth of his attachment to the Mirzā.

"My master, my guide, my leader: *Assalam- o- Alaykum wa Rahmat ullah,*

"It is my prayer to be ever present before you and to learn from you all that for which the Imam of the age has been made the Mujaddid. If it is permitted, I would resign my job and spend day and night in your exalted service; or if it is ordered, I would give up my present engagements and go around the whole world, summoning people towards the true religion and would lay down my life in this cause. I am a martyr in your cause: whatever I have is not mine; it is yours. Respected guide and mentor, with utmost sincerity I say that if all my wealth and belongings are sacrificed in the cause of religious preaching, I will have achieved my purpose. If the buyers of Barahin in advance are uneasy at the delay in the publication of the book, please permit me to render the humble service of paying them all their dues from my pocket.

"Respected pir and guide: this worthless one, ashamed of himself, says that if this offer is accepted, it would be a pleasure for him. What I mean is that I may be permitted to bear the entire cost of printing Barahin, and that whatever proceeds there might be from its sale, should be spent on your needs. My relationship with you is the same as that of Fariq (with the Prophet), and I am prepared to sacrifice all in this path. Please pray that the end of my life be like that of *Siddiqs* (the truthful ones)."[40]

Nūruddin's faith in the Mirzā was very deep indeed. It so happened that when the Mirzā wrote *Fath-i-Islam* and *Tawdih al-*

---

[40] *Mirqat al- Taqin* and *Hayat- i- Naruddin*, pp. 17-1.

Maram someone asked Nüruddin, before he had seen these books, if any other Prophet could come after the Holy Prophet.

"No", he replied. "And if someone claims to be a Prophet?" he was asked. Nüruddin replied that if someone did claim so, it would be seen whether he was truthful or not; and that his claim would be accepted if he was truthful. After narrating this incident, Nūruddin himself adds:

> "This was just the case of prophethood. My faith is that even if the Promised Messiah were to proclaim himself to be the bearer of a Sharah and abrogate the Quranic Sharah, I will not reject that claim. For, when we have accepted him (i.e. the Mirzā) to be truthful and to have been commissioned by God, then whatever he will say will of necessity be true and we will have to think that the (Quranic) verse in respect of *Khatim ol-Nabiyin* (the last of the Prophets) has a different meaning."[41]

During his association with the Court of Jammu, Nūruddin wrote *Fasl-ul-Khitab* in four volumes under the guidance of the Mirzā in which he refuted Christianity. He kept on contributing very magnanimously to the publication of the works of the Mirzā and quite often the Mirzā took large sums of money as loans from him[42] and praised him for his religious enthusiasm, his readiness to help the religious cause and his large-hearted generosity. The famous couplet of the Mirzā about Nūruddin is:

> "How good would it be, were everyone in the Ummat a Nūruddīn;

[41] *Sirat al- Mahdi*, pp. 98-99.

[42] *Maktübat- i- Ahmadiyah*, Vol. V, See Letters to Nüruddin.

That would be so, if the light of faith burnt in the heart of everyone."[43]

For several reasons, particularly the intrigues of the courtiers, the Mahārājā's attitude towards Nūruddin subsequently changed. In 1893 or 1894, his service with the Mahārāja was terminated and Nūruddin returned to Bhaira. After a brief stay and practice of medicine there he moved to Qadian permanently and dedicated his life to supporting the Mirzā and spreading his movement.

Accession to Khilafat

On the Mirza's death on May 26, 1908, he became his first Khalifah. The followers of the Mirzā paid their allegiance to him, and he was proclaimed to be the "Khalifah of the Promised Messiah", and "Nūruddin the Great." For quite some time, Nūruddin remained hesitant whether he should consider those who did not believe in the Mirza's prophethood to be unbelievers. Later, he was converted to the view that they were unbelievers."[44] There was some controversy about his nomination as the Khalifah. Some people strongly opposed it. On one such occasion, he said:

> "I say by God that it is God Himself who had made me the Khalifah. So, who now has the power to snatch from me the robe (literally the covering sheet) of this Caliphate? It was the Will of God Himself and was in the light of His Own wise consideration, to make me your Imām and Khalifah. You can attribute to me a thousand short comings. They, in fact, will be

---

[43] *Mirqat al- Taqin.*

[44] See Mirzā Bashir Ahmad: *Kalimat al- Fast*, Chapter VI.

attributable not to me, but to God Himself who appointed me the Khalifah."[45]

On another occasion he said:

> "God has made me the Khalifah. Now, neither can I be dismissed (from Caliphate) by your biddance nor has anyone the power to remove me. If you force me any further, bear in mind that I have at my disposal many Khalid ibn Walids who will punish you as (Khalid bin Walid had punished) the apostates."[46]

Nüruddin remained the Khalifah of the Qadiani movement for six years. In 1914, he fell from a horse and died on March 13, 1914. A few days before his death, his tongue had ceased to function.[47] He nominated Mirzā Bashīruddin Mahmood, the eldest son of Mirza Ghulam Ahmad, to be his successor and Khalifah.

Temperament

A study of Nüruddin's life shows that he possessed a mercurial nature and remained a prey to mental conflicts during the greater period of his life. From the very beginning he had a bent towards "free-thinking". First of all, he freed himself from the bonds of the four Muslim schools of jurisprudence and carried his non-conformism to an extreme. Then he came under the influence of Sir Sayyid Ahmad Khan's literature and assimilated his way of thinking. This was the time when some elementary knowledge of physical

---

[45] Review of Religions, Qädian, Vol. 14 No. 6, p. 234 (quoted from Ilyas Barni's Qadiyani Mazhab).

[46] *Tashkhiz al- Azhan*, Vol. 9 No. 11 cited by Barney.

[47] The Daily *Al- Fadhl*, Qädiän, 23 February 1932, (cited from the Qadiani Sect).

sciences was finding its way to India and the rationalists among Indian Muslims were becoming deeply impressed by it. Those who had a religious inclination attempted to harmonise Quranic teachings with scientific knowledge. If this harmonisation presented any difficulty, they tried to overcome it by offering far-fetched interpretations of Quranic verses and the Quranic terminology. Nūruddin's teaching of Tafsir was representative of this intellectual trend.[48]

In Sirat al- Mahdi, Mirzā Bashir Ahmad writes:

"In the beginning Hazrat Nūruddin, the first Khalifah, was deeply under the influence of the way of thinking and the work of Sir Sayyid. But, subsequently, due to contact with Hazrat Sahib, this influence gradually wore off."[49]

But a study of his ideas as well as those of his disciples makes it evident that either because of the influence of Sir Sayyid's ideas, or because of his own predilection he remained the same all his life. His mind had been moulded into a rigid frame, and his mental attitudes had become too hardened to change.

A more careful study of his life reveals that along with his enlightenment and rationalism, there was a strong superstitious element in his personality. Despite all his non-conformism and rationalism, he attached great importance to 'dreams' and 'inspirations'. It has been observed that not infrequently people who stand for intellectual freedom, in fact, for intellectual revolt, also have an inherent trait of superstitiousness. Their frame of mind is

---

[48] A good example of his way of thinking is found in the Tafsir of his pupil Maulavi Muhammad Ali Lahori (His Tafsir is found in English as well as Urdu).

[49] Sirat al- Mahdi, Vol. I, p. 159.

basically apologetic. Such people keep on raising the banner of revolt all their lives against certain institutions or personalities, but, at the same time, when they submit before someone, their power of free-thinking and independent judgement is totally paralysed. Man's life is a strange combination of action and reaction, and his personality a complex of divergent, even mutually conflicting elements. Nothing is more difficult to understand and analyse than the driving urges of a man's personality.

PART II:

On the Road to Prophethood

1: Mirza as Champion of Islam

We have covered so far, a part of the life of Mirza Ghulam Ahmad, his life in his township in district Gurdaspür where we saw him immersed in the study of religious books. His works published after 1880 indicate that the main subjects of his study were different religions, particularly Christianity and Indian religions such as Sanatan Dharma and Arya Samaj.

This period is known for the religious polemics. The educated people of the time had a relish for religious debates and controversies. We have already seen that Christian missionaries were busy propagating Christianity and refuting Islam. The British Government, which was officially the defender of the Christian Faith, patronised these activities, considering India a gift of Jesus Christ. On the other hand, were the preachers of the Arya Samaj movement who were enthusiastically trying to undermine Islam. The British who was aware of the dangerous possibility of inter-communal concord in India, a manifestation of which was the struggle for Indian Independence of 1857, found it expedient to encourage religious controversies. The British political interest was served by these controversies in so far as they led to mutual hatred, intellectual bewilderment, and moral chaos in the country so that the religious communities of India might be disposed at least to tolerate a government which sought to protect all of them and under whose shadow all could carry on their holy debates. In such an atmosphere, anyone why rose to defend Islam and falsify other religions naturally attracted the attention of all Muslims.

The ambitious and far-sighted Mirzā chose this field for his adventures. He undertook to produce a voluminous work to demonstrate, on the one hand, the truth of Islam, the Divine origin of the Qur'an, and the Prophethood of the Messenger of Allah by rational arguments, and to refute Christianity, Sanātan Dharma, Arya Samajand Brahmo Samāj etc., on the other hand. He named this book *Barahin-i-Ahmadiyah.*

The Barahin and the Mirza's Challenge

The writing of Barahin started in 1879.[50] The author undertook to put forward one hundred arguments in support of Islam. In this undertaking the Mirzā also had correspondence with other learned people whom he requested to communicate to him their views in order to help him in this venture. Those who complied with his request included Maulavi Chirāgh 'Alī who was a noted colleague of Sir Sayyid Ahmad Khan. The Mirzā included some of his articles and researches in his work. At long last this work, which was anxiously awaited by hundreds of people, did break into print in four volumes. Along with this book, its author also published an announcement in Urdu and English and sent it to rulers and ministers of States, to Christian clergymen and to Hindu pandits. In this book the Mirzā announced for the first time that he had been appointed by God to demonstrate the truth of Islam and that he was prepared to satisfy the followers of other religions about his religion. The announcement categorically stated:

"This humble slave (the author of *Barahin-i-Ahmadiyah*) has been appointed by the Glorious Almighty to strive for the reform of God's creatures and to show to the ignorant the straight path (which leads to true salvation and by following which the light of heavenly existence and of Divine pleasure and graciousness can be experienced even in this world) in the manner of the Israelite

[50] Sirat al- Mahdi, Vol. II, p. 157.

Prophet of Nazareth (Messiah) with utmost humility and self-denial, self-abasement and gentleness. It is for this purpose that *Barahin-i-Ahmadiyah* has been written, of which thirty-seven parts have been published. Its summary is to be found in the announcement enclosed with this letter. But since the publication of the whole book would require a long time, it has been decided that this letter along with the English announcement should be published and one copy of each sent to the honourable priests of Punjab, India and England and other countries wherever possible."[51]

The Mirzā challenged the world to come forward with any book parallel to this one and invited the representatives of other religions to prove the truth of their religions by the same or even lesser number of arguments than he had put forward. He wrote:

"I, the author of this book, *Barahin-i-Ahmadiyah*, make this announcement with the promise to make a reward of 10,000 rupees to the followers of all faiths and religions who deny the truth of the Glorious Qur'an and the Prophethood of Hazrat Muhammad Mustafa (God's benediction and salutation be on him) and in support of it I commit myself to a formal legal undertaking and a Shara'i pledge that if any of these deniers can show that their scriptures have as many and as sound arguments as found in the Holy Qur'an and which we have mentioned herein to demonstrate the truth of the Glorious Message and the veracity of the Apostleship of the *Khātim-al-Ambiya* (God's benediction and salutation be upon him), which have been derived from the Sacred Book (Qur'an) itself; or if they cannot come forward with an equal number of arguments, then half, or a third, or a fourth, or fifth of the number of our arguments; or if they find that impossible, then at least to refute our arguments one

[51] Supplement to *Barahin- i- Ahmadiyah*, Vol. I by Merajuddin Umar, p. 82

by one- then, in either of these cases, provided three authors accepted by both the parties, unanimously express the view that the condition has been fulfilled in the manner it should have been fulfilled-the announcer (of this announcement) shall hand over to such a respondent without an excuse or hestitation the occupancy and ownership of his property valued at Rs. 10,000."[52]

The Mirzā called upon the Muslims to make monetary contributions to this great service which he wanted to render to the cause of Islam and to participate in it generously.[53] It seems that the response of Muslims to this call was not as enthusiastic as the Mirzā had expected. In the later volumes of Barahin he has mourned their lack of enthusiasm.[54]

The announcements which formed the preface of the book are significant. In them we find some indications of the driving forces of the Mirzā's personality. In them we notice his habit of boastfulness and self-adulation and his confidence in 'heavenly signs' as means of establishing his claims and persuading people. Along with all that, the statements unmistakably smack of his commercial mentality.

Preaching and Politics

In the third and fourth volumes of *Barahin-i-Ahmadiyah*, the Mirzā openly praised the British government and enumerated at length its acts of benevolence towards Muslims in the sections entitled, 'An Important Appeal to Islamic Associations: The Precarious Condition of Muslims and the English Government.' In this appeal he urged all Islamic Associations to prepare a joint

---

[52] Barahin- i- Ahmadiyah, Vol. I, pp. 17-22.

[53] See Iltimās-i-Zaruri in Brakin, Vol. I.

[54] Arz- i- Zurüri ba Halat- i- Majburl. Brāhin, Vol. I.

memorandum and send it to the government with signatures from all prominent Muslims. He also reiterated the services rendered by his family to the British and stressed the impermissibility of jihad.

Thus, we find that even the first work of the Mirzā was not free from panegyrics to the British government, or from political admonitions to the Muslims to remain loyal to the British.

The Magnum Opus

The Mirzā worked on this book from 1880 to 1884. After the publication of the fourth volume, there came a long period of gap, and the fifth and the last volume appeared in 1905, that is, full twenty-five years after the commencement of the work. In the fifth volume, the author mentioned that the publication of the last volume had remained in suspension for twenty-three years. During this period, a large number of people who had paid in advance for all the five volumes but had received only four volumes had passed away. Several other people who had paid in advance had expressed their disapproval and resentment at not receiving the promised volume for which the Mirzā apologized in the fifth volume. In this volume he has also mentioned that previously he had in mind to bring forward 300 arguments to prove the truth of Islam, but later he gave up the idea. In the same way, instead of fifty, he would bring out only five volumes. The reason for this change of mind was that the difference between the two figures was merely that of a zero. In his own words:

> "Earlier I had thought of writing 50 volumes, but now I have confined myself to writing five since the difference between the figures fifty and five is just that of one dot (that is

zero). Thus, the promise has been fulfilled by the publication of five volumes."[55]

In *Sirat al-Mahdi*, Mirzā Bashir Ahmad writes:

"Now that four volumes of *Barahin-i-Ahmadiyah* have come out in print, its preface and notes all relate to the time of publication, and it contains very little of the original work, that is, not more than a few pages. This can be gauged from the fact that out of the 300 arguments which he had written the *Barahin-i-Ahmadiyah* contains only one argument, and that too not in a complete form."[56]

Anyone who studies *Barahin-i-Ahmadiyah* is bound to be impressed by the author's prolificity, perseverance and diligence. These virtues, at best, could stand him in good stead as a successful debater and and an able writer on religious polemics with Christians and Arya Samājīs. In this huge work, however, one does not find any worthwhile research. Nor does one find that familiarity with the sources of Christianity, its ancient literature, its doctrines and history, and that grasp of its funda- mental concepts as one finds, for example, in the works of Maulānā Rahmatullah Kayrānwi (d. 1309 A.H. / 1891 A.D.), the author of Izhār al-Haqq and Izalat al-Awhām. Nor does one find that sweetness and elegance of expression, and that originality and brilliance of argument that one finds in works such as those of Maulānā Muhammad Qasim Nānawatwi's (d. 1297 A.H./1879 A.D.) Tagrir Dilpizir and Hujjat al-Islām.

---

[55] Preface of *Barahin- i- Ahmadiyah*, Vol. V, p. 7.

[56] Sirat al-Mahdi, Vol. I, p.7.

Inspirations and Bragging

The reader also frequently encounters in the Mirzā's book references to his Divinely inspired revelations, to miracles and to Divine communications and prophecies, and last but not the least, his boastfulness. All this leaves an unpleasant taste in the mouth and transforms the book which claims to embody a sober academic discussion and a dignified religious debate, into a work of personal bragging-a work in which, again and again, the author stoops to self-advertisement and self-glorification.

The central theme of the book is that Divine inspiration had not ceased and should not cease. This inspiration itself is the most powerful proof of the validity of any claim and the truth of religion and faith. Whoever will follow the Holy Prophet perfectly will be endowed with the external and internal knowledge which had been granted originally to the Prophets, and the person will, therefore, become possessed of sure, categorical knowledge. The intuitive knowledge of such people would resemble the knowledge of the Prophets. It is these people who have been called Amthal in Hadith and Siddiq in the Qur'ân. The time of their advent would resemble the time of the advent of the Prophets. It is such people who will establish the truth of Islam and their inspiration will be of a categorical nature.[57] In trying to prove the continuity of this inspiration, he cites his own inspirations and writes:

> "We have several examples of this inspiration before us. But in the one which took place just now at the time of writing these notes in March 1882 it has been revealed as a prophecy that through this book and on becoming informed of its contents, the opponents will ultimately be defeated; that

[57] *Barahin-i-Ahmadiyah*, Vol. III, p. 231 and 244.

> seekers after Truth will find true guidance; perversion of belief will be uprooted; and people will help and turn their attention and come around (me) etc., since God will put this into their hearts and direct them to it...[58]

This has been followed by a more recent lengthy inspiration which is almost an entirely incoherent collection of different Quranic verses. This inspiration embraces about forty lines of the Barahin and contains about fifty-three or fifty-four Quranic verses, interspersed with a few Traditions of the Prophet. Besides, there are a few sentences by the Mirzā himself which are an example of what might be termed as poor Indianized Arabic. The last lines of the inspiration which contain a comparatively smaller proportion of Quranic verses, read as follows:

> "Live in the world like a stranger or traveller. Become one of the righteous and the truthful. Bid whatever is good and forbid whatever is bad and send your salutations to Muhammad and his progeny. Prayer alone brings man up. Verily I will raise thee towards Myself, and I have put love from Me (in the hearts of people). There is no god but Allah. So, write and let it be published and sent to the world. Grasp Unity (of God), Unity (of God), O people of Iran and give glad tidings to those who believed that they have a standing with their Lord. And read out to them what has been revealed to thee from thy Lord. And do not swell thy face for the creatures of God and do not get tired of people. The people of al-Suffah. And who are the people of al-Suffah? Thou shalt see their eyes wet with tears and they will send their salutations to thee. O

[58] *Barahin- i- Ahmadiyah*, Vol. III. p. 238.

Lord of ours! We heard a herald calling towards belief, a summon towards Allah, and a bright lamp. Be of hope!"[59]

In the same way, an inspiration has been reproduced in the fourth volume of the same book. This inspiration too is an incoherent conglomeration of Quranic verses and Quranic expressions. It also contains some very obvious errors of Arabic language and grammar (which have been indicated by us by question marks):

> "And when it is said to them believe as men believed, they say: Should we believe as they believe who are stupid? Beware! it is they who are stupid, but they know not, and wish that you should compromise with them (?) Say: Un-believers! I worship not that which you worship. It was said to you: turn to God, but you turn not; and it was said to you, subdue your souls, but you subdue them not. Doest, thou seek of them any reward that feel burdened (in accepting your message). No, we brought Truth to them (gratuitously), and it is Truth to which they are averse. God is pure and free from whatever they attribute to Him. Do people think that they would be left by merely saying: We believed, and they would not be put to any trial? These people love to be praised for deeds which they have not performed, while nothing is hidden from God, and nothing is good which God does not make good and no one can restore him to His favours who has fallen from His grace."[60]

---

[59] *Barahin- i- Ahmadiyah*, Vol. II, p. 242.

[60] *Barahin- i- Ahmadiyah*, Vol. IV, p. 509.

Apart from these revelations in the Arabic language there are two revelations in English as well.[61]

Mirza's beliefs in the Barähin

In the four volumes of Barahin (published 1880-1884), the Mirzā expressed merely the view that *ilham* (Divine inspiration) had not ceased and would not cease, and that the legacy of the Prophets continues in respect of inspired comprehension of things, in respect of the illumination of faith and categorical knowledge. In this book, he has also frequently mentioned that he had been commissioned by God to reform the world and spread the message of Islam; that he was *mujaddid* (renovator) for the present age, and that he bore resemblance to Jesus (peace be on him).[62] In this book he also adheres to the notion of the ascension of Jesus to the heaven and that he would return to the earth. In the appendix to his book, *Nuzül al-Musih*, published in 1902, and in volume V of Barahin, which came out in 1905, the Mirzā has admitted that he used to subscribe to the above view and has even expressed his surprise at his having believed in the ascension and return of Jesus.[63] In Barahin he had also strongly rejected the idea of any fresh revelation and of the advent of any new Prophet. The reason for this belief was that the Qur'an and its teachings were in no danger of being distorted nor was there any danger of Muslims reverting to pre-Islamic ignorance and paganism. On the contrary, he admitted that 'the attitude of the polytheists, owing to contact with the monotheists is gradually tending towards monotheism.' This being the case that the main

---

[61] Ibid, pp. 554 and 556.

[62] Sirat al- Mahdi, Vol, I, p. 39.

[63] Appendix to *Nuzül al- Masih*, p. 6. and Barahin Vol. V. p. 85.

dangers which revelation and prophethood seek to avert were no longer real-there was no need for any new Shari'ah, or any fresh *ilham* (inspiration). This also established the termination of prophethood with the advent of the Holy Prophet:

"Now, since it is rationally impossible and unconceive able that the true teachings of the Glorious Furqan will be distorted or changed, or the darkness of polytheism and worship of God's creatures would predominate again it is also rationally inconceivable that there should be a new Shariah, or the sending down of a new inspiration (*ilhām*). For, that which leads to impossibility is itself also impossible. Thus, it is proved, that the Holy Prophet was in reality the last of the prophets (*Khalim-i-Rusul*)."[64]

Reception of the book

It seems that the book was enthusiastically welcomed in the religious and academic circles of the country. Indeed, the publication of this work was very well-timed and the Mirzā as well as his friends publicised it with great zest. The secret of the success of the book seems to lie in the fact that it challenged other religions and instead of apologising on behalf of Islam it took the offensive against them. Noted among those who appreciated and enthusiastically supported this book was Maulānā Muhammad Husain Batālawi. In his magazine Ishaat al-Sunnah, he wrote a long review eulogising the book in six issues of the magazine.[65] In this review the book was lavishly praised and commended as a great academic achievement of the time, a masterpiece of research and

[64] Barahin, Vol. IV, p. 111 n.

[65] Vol. VII, 1884 nos. 6-11.

authorship. Not much later, the Maulānā felt alarmed at the big claims and 'inspiration' of the Mirzā and, subsequently, became one of his staunch opponents. On the other hand, there were many who were alarmed even by his first book and who began to feel that its author had set himself on a path which would lead him, in the near future, to claim prophethood for himself. Among these far-sighted people were the two sons of the late Maulānā Abdul Qadir Ludhianawi, Maulana Muhammad and Maulānā Abdul Aziz. The Ahl-i-Hadith ulama of Amritsar and some ulama of the Ghaznawī family opposed him from the very beginning and denounced his inspirations as fantasies.[66]

This book brought the Mirzā out of obscurity and put him on the stage of public renown so that countless eyes were turned towards him. In Sirat al-Mahdi, Mirzā Bashir Ahmad has aptly observed how this book brought the Mirzā to the limelight:

"Before writing Barahin, the Promised Messiah spent a life of anonymity and in this isolation, his was the life of a darwish. Before Barahin he had become known to some extent as a result of his having written a series of articles in some newspapers, but all this was very meagre. In fact, it is the announcement of *Barahin-i-Ahmadiyah* which, for the first time and for good, placed him before the country and introduced him to those interested in academic and religious matters. The eyes of the people began to turn in amazement, towards this anonymous villager who had promised to write a great book about the truth of Islam in such a challenging manner and with the promise of a huge sum of money as a reward (to anyone who could refuse his arguments). Thus, the sun of guidance which had already appeared on the horizon, now began to

---

[66] See Isha at al-Sunnah, June, 1884. Vol. VII, No. 6.

rise higher. Later the publication of *Barahin-i-Ahmadiyah* created an extraordinary stir in the religious circles of the country. In general, the Muslims welcomed him as a great *'Mujaddid'*. As for the opponents of Islam, this book came to them as a bombshell and created great turbulence in their camp."[67]

The Mirzā himself says the following about his life before the publication of Barahin:

"This was the time when nobody knew me; when nobody was either in favour of or opposed to me, for, at that time, I was a non-entity; I was just one among the people, hidden in the corner of anonymity."[68]

He adds:

"All the people of this town (i.e. Qādiān) and thousands of other people are aware that at this period of time I was, in fact, like a dead body which had been buried in the grave for centuries and no one even knew whose grave it was."[69]

Debates with Arya Samājis

In 1886, the Mirzā had a debate with Murli Dhar of Arya Samāj in Hoshiarpur. He has written a full-fledged book about this debate, *Surmah-i-Chashm-i-Arya* (Kohl for the eye of the Arya). This is the second of his polemics on religions and religious sects.

The topic of the first day's debate was the rational and historical proof of the miracle of cleaving the moon. The Mirzā not

---

[67] Sirat al- Mahdi, Vol. I, pp. 103-104.

[68] *Tatimmah Haqiqat al- Wahy*, pp. 27-28.

[69] Ibid, p. 28.

only strongly affirmed this miracle but the miracles of other prophets as well. He showed that the occurrence of miracles and super-natural incidents was rationally possible. He took the position that because of the inherent limitations of man's intellect, knowledge and experience, he had no right to deny miracles and thus make the claim to comprehend this vast universe in its entirety. He repeatedly stressed that the knowledge of man was very limited and the range of possibilities very wide[70] (so that the notion that man's knowledge could be comprehensive was untenable). He also stressed that in religious matters faith in the unseen was essential and that this was not in conflict with reason, for the latter could not be all comprehensive in its range. In fact, whatever rational objections the Mirzā pointed out to the belief regarding the ascension of Jesus to the heavens and his descent in future and his stay in the heaven for several centuries and the so-called 'rationalist' trend in his later writings can best be refuted by the arguments that he himself advanced in this book. The personality of the author in this book is quite different from the one in his later writings.

These two books made the Mirzā excessively self-appreciative; he became aware of his ability as a writer and debater and became confident that he was capable of initiating a new movement and influencing his environment. It seems that this discovery proved to be the turning-point in his life. Hence- forth, instead of debating with Christians and Arya Samājis he turned towards Muslims and began to challenge them to debate with him.

---

[70] *Surma- i- Chashm-i- Arya* pp. 557.

2: The Mirza Becomes Messiah

Influence of Nūruddin

We have seen earlier that when Nüruddin was in Jammu in connection with his employment, the Mirzā was staying in Sialkot, where he was employed in the District Commissioner's office. The two had a number of things in common, both relished religions controversies and debates, and both were ambitious. It seems plausible that each of them was influenced by the other's personality. Hence, correspondence between them began in 1885. In the collection of the Mirza's letters, the earliest letter to Nūruddin that we find is dated March 8, 1885. This correspondence continued without break and became so intimate as to include family and matrimonial problems. In January 1888, the Mirzā undertook a trip to Kashmir in order to meet Nūruddin and stayed with him for a month. The Mirzā kept Nūruddin in touch with his inspirations, inspired predictions, and novel pieces of information and research. He even complained to Nūruddin about the opposition of the 'ulama and the alleged view of some of them that he was not a Muslim. In a letter of July 15, 1890, he wrote to Nūruddin: "And I have heard that these people have begun to call me in hushed tones a kafir. It was known from this that the Exalted Allah wants to show something great."[71]

Up till then (i.e. 1890), the Mirza had only claimed, that he was a *mujaddid* and that he had been commissioned by God, and according to Mirza Bashir Ahmad, he continued to say that he had been raised to reform the people in the manner of the Messiah of Nazareth and

---

[71] *Maktübat- i- Ahmadiyah*, Vol. V, p. 79.

that he had a certain resemblance to him.[72] In the Barahin he expressed the opinion that the absolute predominance of Islam which has been promised in the Quranic verse: 'It is He who has sent His Apostle with Guidance and the Religion of Truth to proclaim it over all religions' would be fulfilled through the Promised Messiah, whose return to the world had been mentioned in the Traditions of the Prophet. As for himself, he merely resembled the Messiah in respect of the first phase of his life, that is, his life on earth. In his own words:

"This verse ('It is He who has sent His Apostle') is a prophecy which, in the physical and political senses refers to the Messiah; and the promise of complete predominance of the religion of Islam which has been made will be fulfilled through the triumph of the Messiah. And when Hazrat Masih (upon him be peace) will come into this world, Islam will spread all over the world, to all lands. But it has been revealed to this humble one that in view of his poverty and humility, his trust in God and his sacrifice, and in respect of signs and illuminations, he is an example of the first phase of the life of Messiah and that the natures of this humble one and of the Messiah are extremely alike as if they were two pieces of the same substance, two fruits of the same tree; and the similarity goes to such an extent that the distinction is very minor."[73]

Nuruddin's Advice

In the life of the Mirza as well as in the history of Qadianism, the year 1891 is very crucial. It is in the beginning of this year that Nüruddin, in one of his letters, advised the Mirzā to proclaim

---

[72] Sirat al- Mahdi, Vol. I, p. 39.

[73] *Barahin- i- Ahmadiyah*, Vol. IV, p. 495-98.

himself to be the Promised Messiah.[74] We have not been able to see this letter of Nūruddin, but the reply sent by the Mirzā refers to this advice of Nūruddin. This letter of the Mirzā is included in the collection of his letters and is dated January 24, 1891. This letter reveals the intellectual sources, the behind-the-scenes director of the play, the actual author of Qadianism. The following is an excerpt from this historic letter:

> "It has been said by you, Sir, that there is no harm in proclaiming myself to be the Promised Messiah even independent of the one referred to in the Damascene Hadith. This humble one has no need of becoming a replica of the Messiah. I merely want Allah to include me among His humble and obedient servants. But we cannot escape from being put to test. The Exalted Allah has made trial the only way to advancement, as He says: "Do men think they will be left alone on saying 'We believe, that they will not be tested?[75] (XXIX, 2)

What were the real motives of this advice? Was it merely Nüruddin's far-sightedness and ambitious nature, or had it been made on some kind of encouragement from the powers-that-were? It is difficult now to say what actually lay behind the advice. As for the latter possibility, it appears nor far-fetched at all if we bear in

---

[74] Although in his letter Nüruddin used the expression Replica of the Messiah, the study of *Fath-i-Islam* and *Izalat al-Awham* shows that Replica of the Messiah and Promised Messiah were treated as synonymous terms and were used by the Mirza interchangeably. To cite an instance:
"This descent does not mean the real descent of the Messiah, the son of Mary; it is only a figurative expression which, informs the coming of the one like the Messiah which, according to Divine pronouncements and inspirations, is this humble one."

[75] Maktübat- i- Ahmadiyah, Vol. V, No. 2, p. 85.

mind the historical background of the rise of this new movement. The situation was that the British had witnessed the religious movement of Sayyid Ahmad Shahid and had been put to considerable difficulty owing to that. In more or less the same period of time, there had risen another movement in the Sudan, led by the Sudanese Mahdi, and this too had given the British a very hard time. It is not unlikely that the British should have hit upon the desirability of the rise of a reliable religious leader of their choice. If such a leader was able to win the confidence of the Muslims through his services to the cause of Islam and capture the religious imagination of people by his religious zeal, he could serve as a good means to secure the British against the threat of anti-British religious movements. And since the Muslims already believed in the advent of the Messiah, their acceptance of such a person as the Messiah could not have been ruled out as impossible. Such a Messiah, if he preached loyalty to the powers-that-were in the name of God and Islam, could be of great service to the cause of the British. Nothing, however, can be said with complete certainty. Nevertheless, the above cited letter of the Mirzā remains a significant document and might have the clue to the origin of Qādiānism.

What is worth remembering at this point is that so far as the prophets of God are concerned, their mission does not depend on outside suggestions. They receive revelation from the heaven and are categorically informed of their position and mission. Their hearts are full of conviction and from the very first day they announce and keep on stressing what they believe to be the truth. Neither their own faith, nor their summons, depends upon someone else's drawing their attention towards it. From the very first day they keep on saying:

This am I commanded, and I am the first of those who bow to His Will. (VI: 163)

Belief about Jesus

The return of Jesus is an established article of creed in Islam.[76] Muslims have known this and have believed in it. Traditions from the Prophet mention it and, moreover, owing to the adversity of circumstances the Muslims had developed a mood to expect that

---

[76] The ascension of Jesus to the heavens and his return to the world in the future is one of those beliefs of Muslims which have their basis in Quran and is also proved by Prophetic Traditions, and in which Muslims have believed consistently. Ibn Kathir says that the Prophetic Traditions regarding the return of Jesus are numerous enough to be regarded as one supported by an unbroken chain of transmis sion. Ibn Hajar also quotes Abul Husain Abari in *Fatah-al-Basi* regarding the tawatur of Traditions on this question. Shawkäni has written a treatise just on this subject entitled *Tasdiq fi maja fi al- muntazir wa al-Dajjal wa al-Masih.* None of the important religious personalities has been recorded as denying this belief, not even the *Mutazilah.* Ibn Hazm, in his renowned work *Al-Fisal fi al-Milal wa al-Nihal* writes that this belief is established by the unbroken continuity of transmission. 'I his question has been discussed in detail in. Anwar Shah Kashmiri's Aqidat al-Islam. As for the rational aspect of the question, if one accepts the omnipotence of God and affirms the perfection of His Attributes one can have no reason to doubt the possibility of statements found in those traditions whose authenticity and continuity are established. In an age of such tremendous scientific progress as ours when a number of things which were considered hitherto impossible are taking place before our own eyes, when man-made satellites revolve round the world after every few hours, when man has begun to pace the outer space, the idea that a man should ascend to the heavens and stay there alive for a certain period of time can hardly be regarded as inconceivable. To put forward objections which are based on Greek concepts of astronomy or on other worn-out notions appears palpably childish in this age of scientific advancement.

some great, divinely inspired personality would appear suddenly and set things right for them. As the thirteenth century of *hijrah* drew close to its termination, this state of expectancy became even more intense. Nūruddin, therefore, had reasons to presume that in view of the popularity won by the Mirzā by his religious services his claim to be the Messiah was likely to be accepted by Muslims.

The Mirza accepts the suggestion

The manner in which the Mirzā declined to accept the suggestion made by Nūruddin, and the spirit of humility and piety which he evinced in his letter on that subject are very valuable and add to his prestige. But for anyone who studies his works in a chronological order it is hard to retain this feeling of respect for long. For we find him quite soon accepting the suggestion of Nūruddin-which he had turned down earlier of proclaiming himself to be 'the Replica of the Messiah.[77]

If we survey the works of the Mirzā, they can be very easily divided into two phases. The first phase consists of those works in which he seeks merely to prove the validity of Islam and repudiate other religions. In these works, there is no claim of being the Messiah. This is followed by the phase when he did make that claim, and went on making several other claims about himself, each more boastful and grandiose than the previous one. The first book that he wrote during this phase is Fath-i-Islam, published in 1891, the year which marks a major turning-point in the career of the Mirzā. In this

[77] See *Barahin- i- Ahmadiyah, Surmah- i- Chashm- i- Arya* and *Shahna- i- Haq.*

work we find him claiming to be the Replica of the Messiah and the Promised Messiah.[78]

> "If you are honest, then be thankful and make prostrations of gratitude for this is the time for which your noble forefathers kept waiting until they passed away, the time which was awaited by innumerable souls who have journeyed (to the next world); for, verily, you have found that time. Now it is for you to value it or not, to benefit from it or not. I shall say this again and shall not cease announcing that I am he who has been sent at the proper time in order to reform people so as to revive religion afresh in their hearts. I have been sent in the same way as the one who was sent after Kalim Allah... ...and whose soul, after great many pains during the rule of Herodius, was raised to the heavens. So, when the second Kalim Allah, who, indeed, was the first, and the leader of the Prophets, came for the suppression of other Pharaohs, the one concerning whom it has been said: 'We have sent to you (O men) an Apostle, to be a witness concerning you even as we sent an apostle to Pharoah; (LXXIII: 15) then he too, who is similar to the first Kalim in respect of his work, and yet nobler in rank than he was promised a Replica of the Messiah. And this Replica of the Messiah, having been given the power, nature and characteristics of the Messiah, the son of Mary, descended from the heaven in an age, similar to his age, and

[78] Mirzā Bashir Ahmad writes in Sirat al-Mahdi: "The Promised Messiah had written Fath-i-Islam towards the end of 1890. This is the first treatise in which he mentioned himself to be the Replica of Messiah and that the Messiah of Nazareth had died. In other words, this was the first proclamation of the claim of being the Promised Messiah." (Vol. I, pp. 267-268). This shows that the author too regards 'Replica of Messiah' and 'Promised Messiah' to be synonymous terms.

> around almost the same time that elapsed between the first Kalim and Messiah, son of Mary, i.e. in the fourteenth century. And this descent was spiritual in the same way as after having risen; perfect people come down in order to reform people. And he too came down in a period similar in every respect to the period of the descent of the Messiah, the son of Mary, in order that it might remain a sign for those who understand.[79]

Even though this piece of the Mirza's writing is terribly puzzling and complicated (and perhaps deliberately so), it clearly shows his new claim that he is the 'Replica of the Messiah'; Three of his works, namely *Fath-i-Islam*, *Tuwdih-i- Mazām*, and *Izāla-i-Awhām*, all deal with the same subject and frequently repeat this claim. In *Fath-i-Islam* at another place the Mirzā writes:

> So, aside from the resemblance with other venerable ancestors bestowed on this humble being, there is also a special resemblance with the nature of Hazrat Masih (upon him be peace) and it is because of this resemblance that this humble one was sent after the name of the Messiah in order to shatter to pieces the crucifixion belief. Hence, I have been sent to shatter the cross and exterminate the pigs. I have come down from the heavens-accompanied by angels on my right and left.[80]

In his *Tavdih-i-Maram*, which is his next book after *Fath- i-Islām* he makes this explicit statement:

> With a certain degree of disagreement Muslims and Christians believe that Messiah, the son of Mary was raised

---

[79] *Fath-i-Islām*, pp. 6 and 7.

[80] Ibid., p. 9 n.

from this elemental existence to the heavens and that in some other age he will come down from the heavens. I have written about the error of this notion in my treatise and have also stated that this descent does not mean the actual descent of Messiah, the son of Mary; it is rather a metaphorical expression informing of the advent of a Replica of the Messiah and which on the basis of information and inspiration from God, applies to this humble one.[81]

Fanciful interpretations

Since Nüruddin had a wide knowledge of the Traditions from the Prophet he used to draw the attention of the Mirzā towards the difficulties in justifying his claims and also used to help him in solving those difficulties. The problem as to how to relate the attributes which had been mentioned with regard to the Messiah required extraordinary intelligence. Here are a few examples of this intelligence-and of its having run riot.

The Traditions on which the Mirzā based his claim of Messiahship also mention a number of details relating to the descent of the Messiah. One of these is that the Messiah would descend in Damascus. Now, if the Mirza was the promised Messiah, how could this be justified in the light of the above- mentioned Tradition? It is obvious that. Damascus and Qādiān are far away from one another. Nevertheless, the paradox did not occur to the Mirzā. It is Nuruddin who drew his attention to it. Let us refer once more to the Mirzā himself on this question:

---

[81] Tawdih- i- Maram, p. 2.

"This humble one had so far not occupied himself with trying to find out the signification of this (i.e. Damascus), when a friend and trusted lover, Maulavi Hakim Nüruddin came here to Qadian and he made a request to turn towards God to reveal the significance of Damascus and the two other ambiguous terms which occur in the Tradition concerned in Muslim. Since in those days I was sick, and my mind was incapable of strenuous exertion I was unable to attend to these matters. Only a little bit of effort led to the explanation of a word, that is, the reality of Damascus was revealed to me."[82]

Later, he explains his inspired discovery of the meaning of Damascus in these terms:

> Thus, it should be clear that in the interpretation of the word 'Damascus' it was revealed to me by God that that town has been called Damascus which is inhabited by a people who have the nature of Yazîd, who follow the practices and ideas of the filthy Yazid, in whose hearts there is no love for God and the Prophet, no veneration for the commandments of God, who have become wont to follow their desires, whose enslavement to the commands of the baser self is such that even the blood of the pure and the sacred appears to them as easy and trifling, who do not believe in the Hereafter and for whom the existence of God is a complicated problem which eludes their understanding. And since the physician should come to the sick, it was essential that the. Messiah should appear among such people.[83]
>
> "Thus, 'the descent of the Massiah in Damascus' clearly indicates that there is someone who is a Replica of the

[82] *Izala- i- Awham*, pp. 32-33.

[83] Ibid. pp. 33-34n.

Messiah, who also resembles Husain owing to the resemblance between these two venerable personalities (the Messiah and Husain), and who will descend in order to warn the Yazıdīs for they are akin to the Jews."[84]

Later, he writes "Damascus has been used merely in a metaphorical way.[85] He also adds:

"Then He told me that these people had the nature of Yazıd, and this town (Qariān) is similar to Damascus. So, the Exalted Allah sent this humble one down to this Damascus for a great purpose (at the eastern side, next to the white minaret of the mosque wherein whosoever entered became safe. Blessed is the One who sent me down at this place).[86]

Two yellow sheets

In interpreting the traditions which mention certain details of the descent of the Messiah and in applying them to himself, the Mirzā indulges in great extravagance of imagination, puts forward the most far-fetched meanings, and comes forward with the most ridiculous notions as if he were sure of the absolute gullibility of his readers. For instance, his opponents pointed out that the Traditions on the basis of which he had argued his case and upon which he had based his claim also stated that at the time of his descent the Messiah would be clad in two yellow sheets. Replying to that, he says:

---

[84] Ibid p. 34.

[85] Ibid., p. 34.

[86] Ibid., p. 68.

"I am a permanently sick man. And the two yellow sheets which have been mentioned in the Traditions as those which would be worn by the Messiah when he would come down, these two sheets are with me-and these are, according to the science of interpretation of dreams, two ailments. Hence, one of these sheets is on my upper part so that headache and giddiness and insomnia and palpitation of the heart come to me in the form of fits. The other sheet which is on the lower part of my body is diabetes which has afflicted me for quite a long time so that often I have urinated a hundred times during the night and day, and due to this frequency of urination I am afflicted with all those ailments of debility which generally result from such a disease.[87]

Eastern minaret of Damascus

Traditions from the Prophet also mention the eastern minaret of Damascus as the place where the Messiah would descend. Instead of interpreting it in some other fanciful manner, as was his wont, what he did in this case was to have a minaret constructed in the eastern part of Qadian. He made this decision in 1900, according to Sirat al-Mahdi, and invited people to donate generously.[88] In 1903, he even laid its foundation.[89] Its completion, however, could not take place during his lifetime, and was accomplished by his son Mirzā Bashīruddin Mahmood.

---

[87] Appendices of Arba'in, Nos. 3 and 4, p. 4.

[88] See the announcement regarding the 'Minaret of Messiah', in *Khutba-i-Ilhämiyah*, p. 1.

[89] Sirat al- Mahdi, Vol. II., p. 154.

Satire and ridicule

The three above-mentioned works also crudely reveal the Mirza's bad temper. They are full of satire and ridicule directed against opponents and contain such bitter vituperation that these books can hardly be reckoned among the books befitting the dignity of any serious cause. The style and mode of expression adopted by the Mirzā in these is not even becoming of sober and dignified writers, not to speak of prophets and religious reformers. The manner in which he scoffs at belief in the survival and the return of the Messiah to the earth and at those who subscribe to it reminds one of the types of wit associated with court-jesters rather than with serious intellectuals. Moreover, the kind of debating skill and quibbling which he employs had nothing to do with the prophetic mode of expression. While trying to point out the rational impossibility of the Messiah's survival in the heavens, he writes:

"Among others, one objection is that even if we were to assume that the Messiah did reach the heavens, along with his terrestrial body, then it would force us to admit that that body is bound to be affected in the heavens by the effects of time, like all other human and animal bodies and that this passage of time will inescapably and inevitably lead someday to his death. Thus, in such a case, it will have to be accepted in respect of the Messiah that after having completed his course of life, he must have expired in the heavens[90] and must have been buried in the grave- yard of the

---

[90] In the Mirza's days neither the physical sciences had developed to the present extent nor was man in possession of that extent of empirical knowledge about the outer space and other planets so as to visualise that terrestrial concepts of time and space are not absolute, and that measurements of time and space beyond the gravitational sphere of the earth might be quite different. He, therefore, could neither appreciate the possibility that a thousand years of this world could be

inhabitants of some planet (the possibility of habitation on which is being accepted in the present times). And even if we were to assume his being alive, there can be no doubt that he would by now have become a decrepit old man and will hardly be capable of rendering any religious service. Under such circumstances, his coming down to the earth seems hardly of any consequence except an unavailing botheration."[91]

At other place, he makes the following comment on that part of the Tradition which mentions that the Messiah will "kill the swine."

"Will the excellent task that will be undertaken by the Messiah after he comes down to the earth merely be to go around, accompanied with a pack of hounds, hunting pigs? If this is true, then Sikhs, Chamars and Sansis and Gandils who love pig-hunting have reason to be glad, for they will prosper."[92]

At another place, he makes the following observation about the future descent of the Messiah:

"Watch out lest you are deceived by someone who first boards some balloon and then alights from it in front of you. So,

---

equal to just a moment in some other world, or, that there might be a world which is quite different from our own in respect of change, death, feelings, requisites for survival, etc. Man seems to have the inalienable weakness of having blind faith in the knowledge and information of his own time and tends to deny all that has not been known or experienced till that time. In the words of the Qur'an 'Nay, they charge with falsehood that whose knowledge they cannot compass, even before the elucidation thereof hath reached them." (X: 39)

[91] *Izata- i- Awhām*, pp. 25-26.

[92] Izaal- i- Awhām; p. 21.

beware! Don't mistake such a person for the son of Mary because of your established belief."[93]

At still another place he refers to the same question in the following manner:

> Brethren, this question stood on two legs:
>
> (1) One, the descent of the son of Mary from the heavens with his terrestrial body, towards the end of time. This leg has been broken by the Glorious Qur'an and also some Traditions by informing of the death of the Messiah, son of Mary.
> (2) The second leg was the appearance of the promised Dajjal towards the end of time. Now this leg has been broken into two pieces by the unanimously agreed Traditions of Sahih Muslim and Sahih Bukhari which have been reported by important Companions and also by calling Ibn Sabä to be the promised Dajjal and, at last, by killing him after making him join the body of Muslims. Now that both the legs of the question have been broken, how and with whose support can this corpse which lacks both the legs stand up after these thirteen countries"?[94]

Messiah till, in the end, he concluded that his death had taken place in Kashmir and that it was there that he lay buried. In this connection, according to his wont, he did a lot of hair-splitting which shows the fertility of his imagination even if the level is childish. He has tried to prove that the pronunciation of Kashmir in Kashmiri language is "Kashir", and it appears that this word, in fact, is a compound Hebrew word, composed of 'K' which is used to

---

[93] Ibid., p. 143.

[94] Ibid., pp. 133-34.

denote similarity, resemblance, etc. and of 'Ashir' which in Hebrew means Syria. Thus, the word *'Kāshîr'* in Hebrew meant 'like Syria'. On this basis, the Mirzā went on to add that when Jesus (peace be upon him) migrated from Palestine to that part of India which due to the excellence of weather, agreeableness of its seasons and its greenery and freshness had close resemblance to Syria, God named it "*Kāshir*" in order to comfort and gratify him. The excessive use of the word led to the dropping of 'a' with the result, that it became 'Kashir.' Then, he proved that the tomb of *'Budhasaf'* (popularly known as the "prince") in the Khān Yar locality of Srinagar was in fact the grave of Jesus. In trying to support this piece of research, he marshalled all possible far-fetched arguments, with the result that his writing on the point appears closer to poetry and fiction rather than what is normally considered to be academic writing. The unbridled speculations of the Orientalists, who are noted for making the mountain out of a molehill simply pale into insignificance when compared with the Mirza's writings.[95]

This brings us to a definite milestone in the spiritual experences and claims of the Mirzā. At this stage he categorically claims to be the "Promised Messiah," and tries to prove this by his so-called 'rational' as well as traditional arguments.

---

[95] See Barahin, p. 228.

3: From Messiah to Prophet

An objective, but critical study of the Mirza's writings gives one the impression that his claims proceeded along a gradually ascending scale. All this seems to have been planned very carefully, and the Mirzā appears to have exercised great patience and precaution in moving from one stage to the other. In the beginning, he expressed the opinion that inspiration, intuitive experience, and categorical knowledge were an essential concomitant of completely following the Prophet - a natural stage at which one arrives as a result of losing oneself in obedience to the Prophet. He does not explicitly claim himself to be a prophet but talks about prophetic attributes and characteristics and tries to prove that these attributes and characteristics are bestowed upon the followers of the Prophet, particularly upon the more perfect ones, by virtue of their following the Prophet. This logic and its premises were bound to lead the Mirzā, sooner or later, to proclaim himself to be a prophet. It appears that throughout these years, he remained busy paving the way and trying to create the proper atmosphere for such a proclamation. He seems to have been trying to assess whether the devotion of his followers had reached the stage where they would not mind accepting even this claim, as they had accepted the rest of his claims.

Proclamation of Prophethood

At last, that event did take place. In the year 1900, Maulavi 'Abdul Karim, the preacher of the Friday sermon, gave a sermon in which he used the words Nabi (Prophet) and Rasül (Messenger) for the Mirzā. This caused great irritation to Maulavī Sayyid Muhammad Ahsan Amrohawi. When Maulavi 'Abdul Karim came to know of this, he gave another Friday sermon in which he addressed the Mirzā, requesting him to contradict his belief, if he was wrong in considering him to be a prophet and messenger of God. After the Friday prayers were over, Maulavi 'Abdul Karim caught hold of the skirt of the Mirza's apparel and requested him to correct him in his beliefs if they were erroneous. The Mirzā turned around and said that he, too, held the same belief. Meanwhile, Maulavī Muhammad Ahsan had been greatly agitated by the sermon and in anger was pacing the floor of the mosque. On Maulavi Abdul Karim's return, he began to quarrel with him. When their voices rose very high, the Mirzā came out of his house and recited the Quranic verse: "O ye who believe! Don't raise your voice above the voice of the Prophet."[96] (XLIX.2)

Thus, the sermon of Maulavi 'Abdul Karim inaugurated a new phase in the career of the Mirzā. This sermon provided him with the much-needed assurance that his followers had such an unquestioning faith in him that they would accept whatever claims he might make. The Mirza's own son, Bashīruddin Mahmood has very ably described this development by pointing out that the Mirzā used to claim his self to be invested with the attributes which could be found in none except a prophet and yet he used to deny his being a prophet. When he became conscious of this inconsistency and became aware that these attributes were untenable with his denial of prophethood, he pro- claimed himself to be a prophet. He writes:

"In short, since in the beginning the Promised Messiah thought that the definition of Nabi is the one who brings a new Shariah, or

---

[96] This event is based on the report of a speech of Sayyid Sarwar Shāh Qadiani at an annual conference held in Qădiăn, and published in ai- Fadhl, Vol. X, No. 51, dated January 4, 1923. See also *Haqiqat al- Nubuwat,* p 124.

abrogates some injunctions, or is a prophet directly (appointed by God): so, even though all the attributes and qualities required of a prophet were found in him, he used to decline from designating himself a prophet. When, later on, he became aware that the nature of his claims is that of a prophet and not of a Muhaddath, he proclaimed himself to be a prophet."[97]

However, whether the Mirzā refrained from proclaiming himself to be a prophet till his misunderstanding was removed and he was commissioned by God to proclaim his prophethood, or he had been waiting all this while for an opportune moment to make this declaration, there is no doubt that he was ultimately led to making the proclamation of his prophethood which was the logical result of his earlier claims.

Elucidation and Challenge

As stated by Mirzā Bashîruddin Mahmood, the question was finally decided in 1901, and the Mirzā began to write about it explicitly in his writings. The collection of articles called Arbain[98] is full of declarations and explanations about this new mission. This frankness increased steadily. In 1902, he wrote a treatise entitled *Tuhfut al-Nadwah*, which was addressed to the ulama who were taking part in the deliberations of the Nadwah Conference held at Amritsar in 1902. In this treatise, he wrote:

"Thus, as I have repeatedly said, what I recite unto you is categorically and certainly the word of Allah, in the same way as

---

[97] *Haqiqat al- Nubüwat*, Vol. I, p. 124.

[98] The Mirza had promised to write forty treatises on the subject, but he concluded the series only after the fourth one. See Arba'in, Vol. IV, p. 14.

Qur'an and Torah are the words of Allah, and that I am a *Zilli*[99] and *Buruzi*[100] prophet of God, and every Muslim is obliged to obey me in religious matters. And everyone who has received information about me, even though he be a Muslim, but does not consider me arbiter in his affairs, nor recognizes me as the Promised Messiah, nor considers my revelations as coming from God; he is liable to punishment in the heavens for he has rejected what he had to accept at its proper time. I do not merely say that I would have courted (the disaster of) death had I been a liar; I also say that I am true even as Moses and Jesus and Muhammad (peace and blessings of Allah be on them) were true, and that God has shown more than ten thousand signs to uphold my claim. The Messenger of Allah (peace and blessings of Allah be on him) has testified and the earlier prophets had indicated the time of my advent, which is the present time. The Qur'an has also indicated the time of my debut during the present times. Both the heavens and the earth have borne testimony in my support; nor is there a prophet who has not testified in my favour."[101]

In the same vein is what he wrote in *Haqiqat al-Wahy*:

"So, of all the people of this ummah, I am the only one who has received this large portion of Divine revelation and knowledge about the Unseen. None of the saints of this ummah, who have

---

[99] Reception of the revelation through the grace of Muhammad (peace be on him) has been called "*Zilli nubüwah*" by the Mirzā. See *Haqiqat al-W'aky*, p. 28.

[100] This kind of prophet, according to the Mirzā does not receive it (i. e. prophethood) for his own self, but for the majesty of his prophet. It is for this reason he claims, that his name in the heavens is Muhammad and Ahmad. This means that the Prophet Muhammad's nubüwah was received ultimately by (another) Muhammad. although ina buruzi way, and not by any body else". Ek Ghalti ka Izālah, p. 5.

[101] Tuhfat al- Nadwah, p. 4.

preceded me, was given such a big share of this bounty.[102] For this reason I alone was chosen to be appointed a prophet, and no one else deserved this title."[103]

All the later writings of the Mirzā are full of similar categorical elucidations of his claim to prophethood. These are too many to be mentioned in this book. All those interested in a more detailed study of it should study his *Haqiqat al-Wahy*, and Bashiruddin Mahmood's *Haqiqat al-Nubuwat.*

Independent Prophethood

The works of the Mirzā also prove that he believed himself to be an independent prophet and bearer of a Shariah. In *Arbain,* he defined the Shariah-bearing prophet as one whose revelation contains positive commandments and prohibitions and who makes some regulations even though these commandments and prohibitions might have been embodied in the scripture of some former prophet. According to him, a Shariah-bearing prophet need not bring an altogether new set of laws. Then he goes on to declare himself to be such an independent Shariah-bearing prophet. To cite his own words.

"Apart from this, you should know what is Shariah. Whosoever laid down some commandments and prohibitions through his revelation and framed some regulations for the ummah becomes the bearer of a Shariah. So, even according to this

[102] This is merely a claim, and it is based on lack of religious knowledge and is against historical facts. In the Ummah of Mohammad (peace be on him) there have been so many saints who have been graced by divine inspiration, but none ever claimed it to be a revelation, nor claimed prophethood on that basis.

[103] Haqiqat al- Wahy, p. 391.

definition, our opponents are blameworthy, for my revelations contain commandments as well as prohibitions. For instance, take the inspiration:

'Say to the believers to lower down their eyes and guard their hidden places-This is purer for them.' (xxv1.30)

"All this is found in *Barahin-i-Ahmadiyah.* It contains commandments as well as prohibitions, and the same is the case with my revelations till today, they contain both commandments and prohibitions. And if you say that by Shariah is meant that which contains new regulations, then this is wrong. The Exalted Allah says: 'And this is in the Books of the earlier Revelations; the Books of Abraham and Moses;' (LXXXVII, 18-19) which means that the Quranic teachings are also embodied in Torah."[104]

The fact that the Mirzā abrogated a number of those important and categorical injunctions of the Shariah, which have been continuously supported by Muslims, also shows that he considered himself to be the bearer of an independent Shariah and regarded himself as one entitled to determine what was religiously obligatory or prohibited. One of the examples is the attitude he took in respect of the question of jihad. Even though jihad is a textual Quranic injunction supported by the unbroken belief and practice of the ummah throughout the fourteen centuries of our history and is supported by the Prophetic Tradition: 'jihad will continue till the Day of Resurrection,' but the Mirzā prohibited it. In connection with the abrogation of *jihad*, just one excerpt from his writings on the subject will suffice:

---

[104] *Arbain*, appendix 4, p. 7.

"*Jihad* that is the harshness of religious wars-has gradually been lightened by God. During the time of Moses there was such harshness that even acceptance of belief could not save a man from being killed, and even suckling babies were put to death. Then during the time of our Prophet (peace and blessings of Allah be upon him) the killing of the children, the old and womenfolk was prohibited. Then, for certain nations, instead of accepting the faith, payment of *jizyah* was accepted as the means of saving them from punishment. Then, in the time of the Promised Messiah, the injunction of jihad has been absolutely repealed."[105]

Excommunication of the Deniers of Mirza's Prophethood:

The natural and logical consequence of the claim to be a prophet was that all those who declined to believe in the new prophethood should be declared unbelievers (kāfirs). The Mirzā himself recognized that only a Shariah-bearing prophet was entitled to declare all those who did not believe in him to be kāfirs. He writes:

> "This point is worth remembering that to call those who reject one's claim as kāfirs is worthy only of those prophets who bring from God a Sharah and new injunctions. But all others besides the Shaah-bearing (prophets), that is, *mulham* (Divinely-inspired) and *muhaddath* (recipients of Divine Communication), no matter how high their station is in the sight of God and no matter how highly honoured they are

[105] *Arba'in*, Vol. 4, p. 15n. For more detailed statements of the Mirzā on the subject see Section 2 of Chapter III of the book.

by God, rejection of their claim does not render anyone an unbeliever."[106]

Nevertheless, all the subsequent works of the Mirzā are replete with denunciations of those who denied his Prophethood as *kāfirs*. A few examples will suffice:

> "During these days the foundation of a new sect will be laid in the heavens and in order to support this sect, God will blow (His trumpet) "Be" and by the sound of this "Be", every fortunate one will be drawn towards it except those who are eternally doomed and have been created to fill up the Hell."[107]

In his inspiration which the Mirza published on May 25, 1900, he said:

> "I have received inspiration that whosoever will not follow thee and will not enter into thy oath of fealty then such a disobeyer of God and the Prophet will dwell in Hell."[108]

Take another instance: "God had revealed to me that everyone who has received my call and has not accepted it is not a Muslim."[109]

At another place, the matter has been dealt with in greater detail:

"Kufr denotes two categories (of disbelief): first, that a person denies Islam itself and does not recognize the Holy Prophet

---

[106] Tiryāq al- Qulub, p. 130n.

[107] Barahin- i- Ahmadiyah, Vol. V, pp. 82-83.

[108] Alivar al- Akhar, p. 8 (cited from Qadiani Mazhab).

[109] Zikr al-Hakim, No. 2, p. 24, compiled by Dr. Abdul Hakim, quoted from al-Fadhl January 15, 1935.

(peace and blessings of Allah be on him) to be the messenger of God. The second (category of) disbelief is, for instance, that he does not believe in the Promised Messiah and considers him false in spite of the matter having been made clear and even though God and the Prophet had emphatically urged that he be recognized as true, and there had been similar emphatic instruction in the books of the earlier prophets. Thus, since he is the denier of the command of God and His Prophet, he is a kāfır. And if one were to look at the matter closely, both these categories of kufr are basically the same; for, the person who does not accept the command of God and His Prophet despite his having recognized it to be so, he does not believe in God and the Prophet according to the explicit texts of the Qur'an and the Hadith.[110]

This constitutes an article of the Qadiani creed. Its former head, Mirzā Bashiruddin Mahmood writes:

"All those Muslims who have not been integrated in the oath of fidelity to the Promised Messiah, regardless of whether they had heard his name or not, they are kāfirs and outside the fold of Islam.[111]

It is because of this belief that all non-Ahmadis are kāfirs, the Islamic legal ordinances in respect of kafirs have been considered by the Qādiānī group to be applicable to those who are outside the fold of their religion. The Qadiānīs have, there- fore, been prohibited from having matrimonial relations with Muslims. In one of his speeches, Mirzā Bashiruddin Mahmood observed: "One of the ordinances of the Promised Messiah, and an important one too is that no Ahmadi may give his daughter in marriage to a non-Ahmadi.

---

[110] Haqiqat al- Wahy, pp. 179-80.

[111] Aina- i- Sadaqat, p. 35 (cited from the Qadiani Sect).

This ordinance is mandatory for every Ahmadi.[112] In Anwar-i-Khilafat he remarks: "A person asked him (i.e. Mirza Ghulam Ahmad Qadianı) again and again and put forward several pressing difficulties. Nevertheless, he instructed him to keep his daughter at home for all her life, but not to give her in marriage to a non-Ahmadi. When after the Mirza's death the said person married his daughter to a non-Ahmadi, the first Khalifah, Hakim Nüruddin, not only forbade him from acting as an Imām of the Ahmadis but also excommunicated him from the Ahmadi group, and did not accept his repentance during the six years of his Khilafat despite his repeated apologies and repentance."[113]

Elaborating on the same theme at another place, he goes on to say:

"The position of non-Ahmadis in relation to us is the same as that fixed for the *ahl-al-kitab*[114] in relation to a believer by the Wise Qur'an, which instructs that a believing man may marry an *ahl-al-kitab* woman, but may not give a believing woman in marriage to an *ahl-al-kitab*. Likewise, an Ahmadi may bring a non-Ahmadi woman into the fold of his marriage; but an Ahmadi woman, according to the Islamic Shariat, may not be given in marriage to a non- Ahmadi male. Huzur (the Mirzā) says: There is no harm in accepting a non-Ahmadı woman in marriage, for marriage with *ahl-al-kitab* women is permitted. Rather, such a marriage is useful, because thus one more person receives true guidance, (but) one should not marry one's daughter to any non-Ahmadi. If you can have (a non-Ahmadı

[112] Barkat- i- Khilafat, Collection of Speeches of Mirzā Bashiruddin Mahmood, p. 15, (quoted from Qadiani Mazhab)

[113] Anwar- i- Khilafat, pp. 93-94.

[114] A follower of one of the revealed religions that is, a Jew or a Christian.

woman), take her. But to give away (an Ahmadi woman in marriage to a non- Ahmadi) is sinful."[115]

In the same way, to pray behind a non-Ahmadı is not permissible. The Mirzā himself wrote:

"This Divine Message shows that those who declare (the Mirzā to be) kafir and adopt the path of falsification (of the Mirzā) are a doomed people. Hence, they do not deserve that any one of my jamaat (group) pray behind them. Can anybody offer prayers behind someone who is dead? So, keep in mind that, as God has informed me, it is prohibited for you, it is absolutely prohibited for you to pray behind anyone who declares (me to be) *kāfir* or falsifies (me), or is hesitant (to follow me)."[116]

Pursuing this logic, participation in the funeral prayers of the Muslims too has been prohibited for the Qâdiānīs. According to the Qâdiānī mouthpiece al-Fadhl 'the Mirzā did not offer prayer at the funeral of his son (late Fadhl Ahmad) because he was a non-Ahmadi.[117] Mian Bashiruddin Ahmad, in a letter published in al-Fadhl, even goes so far as to say: "I believe that it is not permissible to offer prayers at the funeral of those who pray behind non-Ahmadis, for, such a person, in my view, is not an Ahmadi."[118] He also expressed the view that it is not permitted to offer prayers at the funeral of even a non-Ahmadi infant. The argument was that just as prayers could not be offered at the funeral of a Christian child, even

[115] al- Hakam, April 14, 1908 (cited in Qadiani Mazhab)

[116] Arba'in, Vol. III, p. 34n.

[117] Al-Fadhl dated 15th December, 1921.

[118] Al- Fadhl, dated 13th April 1926.

though he was innocent, one could not offer prayers at the funeral of a non-Ahmadi child.[119]

It was in compliance with this injunction, that even though Chowdhry Sir Zafrullah Khan, then Pakistan's Minister for External Affairs, was present at the funeral ceremony of Mr. Jinnah, he did not participate in the funeral prayers.

One of the corollaries of accepting this belief is that whatever religious duties one had performed prior to entering into the fold of Qadianism, would be deemed to be all null and void. In reply to a query raised by a Qadiani, he was informed: "Whosoever performed his obligatory pilgrimage at the time when his (i.e. the Mirzā's) claim had become well- known and the proof of its validity had been made evident to the people of the country in general, and the Mirzā had interdicted praying behind a non-Ahmadī Imām, then that person's Hajj will not be reckoned as having been performed by him."[120]

Incarnation and transmigration of the soul

Some of the writings of the Mirzā indicate that he also believed in the doctrines of incarnation and transmigration of souls and that the souls and essence of the prophets (upon all of them be the peace of Allah) were embodied in the person of the prophets one after another. In *Tiryāqal-Qulub,* he writes:

"Thus, as has been accepted by the Sufis, the levels of existence are cyclical. In this way, Abraham (upon him be peace) was re-born in respect of nature, temperament, and familiarity of heart, two thousand and five hundred years after his death in the house of

---

[119] Al- Fadhl, Vol. 9, No. 72 and Vol. X, No. 32.

[120] al- Hakam, (Qādian) of May 7, 1934.

Abdullah, the son of 'Abd al-Muttalib, and was called by the name of Muhammad."[121]

He also writes:

"At this place, this point needs to be remembered that during the periods of the internal degeneration of Islam, the spirituality of our Prophet (upon him be the peace and benediction of Allah) manifests itself, and this incarnation of the essence of Muhammad shows itself in the form of some perfect follower. As for what has been reported in the Traditions that al-Mahdi would be born and that 'his name would be my name and his mode of conduct be (like) my mode of conduct'-if these Traditions are correct, then the reference is to the descent of his spirit as I have mentioned above."[122]

In another of his works, he wrote:

"It has been made known to me through *kashf* that when Jesus was informed about this sacrilegious which has spread from the Christian people to the whole world, his soul moved for spiritual descent. Thereafter, God, according to His promise, granted him his replica, and in it was infused the Messiah's courage and character and spirituality, and the two-that is, the Messiah and his replica-were firmly integrated as if they were two parts of the same matter. Thus, in this sense, his being became the being of the Messiah, and the yearnings of the Messiah descended into him - and it is the descent of these which, in inspirational terminology, has been described as the descent of the Messiah."[123]

---

[121] Tiryaq al- Qulub, p. 155 n.

[122] Aina i- Kamalat- i- Islam, p. 346.

[123] Ibid., pp. 254-55.

Two advents of the Prophet

The Mirzā also declared that the Holy Prophet (peace and blessings of Allah be on him) has had two advents. He said: "And know that our Prophet (peace and blessings of Allah be on him), in the same way as he was sent in the fifth millennium, was also sent towards the end of the sixth millennium, in the form of the Promised Messiah."[124]

He even felt that this second advent was stronger, more perfect, and brighter than the first one:

"Rather the truth is that his spirituality (upon him be peace) at the end of the sixth millennium, that is, in these days, is more vigorous and stronger and more perfect than 5330 in those years; rather, it is like the full moon."[125]

Mirza's boastfulness

The boastfulness of the Mirzā in respect to his prophethood and his attainments is a noteworthy feature of his life. This reflects a particular kind of psychological complex, and we need not try to analyse it. However, his urge to express his greatness was so pressing that he proclaimed himself to be of the same status as all other prophets. To quote one of his couplets:

He who gave the cup to every prophet,

Gave it to me filled to the brim!

---

[124] Khutba- i- Ilhāmiya, p. 180.

[125] Ibid., p. 181.

Later, he proclaimed himself to be possessed of the virtues of all prophets. To quote him again:

Although prophets there have been many,

In Divine inspiration I am not less than any.[126]

He, further, went on to claim:

Every prophet became alive when I was raised.

Every Apostle lies hidden beneath my garment.[127]

Not only this; he proclaimed that it was he who had brought about the perfection of the human race; that without him, but this garden of humanity was also incomplete:

The garden of Adam which had been incomplete so far,

Has now burst into bloom, complete with leaves and fruit.[128]

He also seems to believe that the attainments of prophethood and spirituality evolve with the passage of time so that these attainments had found their most perfect form in his own personality. He wrote:

"In the same way, the spirituality of our Prophet (peace and blessings of Allah be on him) appeared in the fifth millennium-and that time was not the apex of its advancement-but the first step towards the highest point of its perfection. Then that spirituality radiated itself towards the end of the sixth millennium, that is, during the present time, in the same way as Adam was created towards the end of the sixth day by the command of Allah, the Best

---

[126] Khutba- i- Ilhamiya, p. 99.

[127] Ibid., p. 100.

[128] Barahin- i- Ahmadiya, Vol. V, p. 113.

Creator. And the spirituality of our Prophet, the best of the prophets, made its manifestation in a member of his ummah so that this spirituality might reach the perfection of its manifestation and predominance of its light, as God had promised in his Radiant Book. So, I am that promised manifestation; I am the promised Light."[129]

In Ajāz-i-Ahmadi, he even tries to place his miracles and signs above those of the Holy Prophet. He says: For him, the moon was cleaved, but for me, both the sun and the moon were eclipsed. So, will they still deny?[130]

These boastful claims of the Mirzā provided sufficient ground for his staunch followers and successors to build further on that foundation, as has always happened in the history of sects and religions. It is no surprise, therefore, that many of his followers explicitly declare him to be superior to most of the prophets. Mirzā Bashiruddin Mahmood, the son and second successor of the Mirzā, wrote the following:

"Many prophets have passed in the world, but their disciples did not go beyond the stage of *muhaddath*, except for our Prophet (i.e. Muhammad), whose benediction became so effluent that besides many *muhaddath*, one achieved even the status of prophethood. And it is not only that he became a prophet but having attained perfection by way of reflection of the one whom he followed, went even ahead of some of the great prophets."[131]

---

[129] Khutba- i- Ilhamiya, pp. 177-78.

[130] Ajāz-i-Ahmadi, p. 71.

[131] Haqiqat al- Nubuwat, p. 257.

The enthusiastic followers of Mirzā Bashiruddin, however, did not stop even at that. The mouthpiece of the movement, al-Fadhl, wrote:

"The Promised Messiah was a prophet. His position by virtue of his status, was that of the disciple and the reflection of the Noble Messenger (upon him be peace and blessings of Allah). As for other prophets (upon them be peace), he excelled many of them; may be, he excelled them all."[132]

---

[132] al- Fadhl, Vol. XIV, No. 85, dated April 29, 1927 (cited in Qadiani Mazhab).

PART III: Some Aspects of Life and Character

1: Mirza's Life after the Spread of his Message

Early Life

Mirza Ghulam Ahmad had started his life in poverty. In the early part of his life the situation was that a big part of his landed property had already gone and there was no other means of income. In his own words, he was concerned only with the dining table and the bread.[133] Prior to the spread of his fame he had spent twenty five years of anonymity. To cite own words again: "In fact during this period I was like a dead body, buried for centuries in such a manner that it was not even known whose grave it was."[134] This state of affairs lasted until the appearance of the Mirzā as an author and champion of Islam. Then, his fame spread as a preacher and spiritual leader. He claimed to be the "Promised Messiah", and, subsequently, an independent messenger of God. In this phase, things changed for him. We see him from now on as the spiritual guide and leader of a nascent religious community and a prosperous group of people. Gifts poured in from all sides and he became the centre of adoration and love of thousands of people. It is obvious that the Mirzā's prosperity in this period of his life owed itself to his religious movement. It is religious sentiment alone which led the people to make sacrifices in order to help the Mirzā financially. The student is bound to feel curious as to the effect of this changed circumstance upon his life and character. The Mirzā had risen in the name of a great religious cause and had come forward with the highest possible religious claims about himself. How far was his life in conformity with the ideals of this cause and the big claims he made

---

[133] *Nuzül- al- Masih*, Ist Edition, p. 118.

[134] *Taimmah Haqiqat al- Wahy*, p. 28.

about himself? Making a comparison between him and the noble life of the Holy Prophet Muhammad (peace be upon him) would be sheer insolence. What can possibly be done is to compare his life and character with those followers of the Holy Prophet who have championed the religious cause of Islam and have won popular admiration among Muslims as their true spiritual leaders.

Character of Religious Reformers

A study of the history of inspiring religious personalities and dynamic religious movements in Islam makes one thing quite evident. Even while experiencing fame and the availability of material riches these noted religious personalities showed tremendous indifference towards worldly ambitions, an admirable sense of self-contentment and great sacrifice, and an ever mounting keenness to strive for nothing except the felicity of the next life. The entire life of such people was subordinated to the conviction that the next life constitutes the real life. Their motto seems to have been the saying of the Prophet: "O God there is no life except the life of the Hereafter." They passed through worldly life the way a traveller passes through the various stages of his journey, always keeping the following saying of the Holy Prophet before their eyes:

"What is my concern with the world? My relation to world is similar to that of a rider who stays (for a while) under the shade of a tree, then gets up and leaves."[135]

Their life embodies, to an appreciable degree, the following description of the life of Hazrat Ali (may Allah be pleased with him), by one of his friends:

---

[135] Reported in Ahmad, Tirmidhi and Ibn Majah.

"He was weary of the world and its bloom and loved night and its darkness. He was, by God, profuse in tears, immersed in reflection, wondering at the march of time, always critically watchful of himself (literally, always addressing his soul). The dress that pleased him was the rough one; and the food that pleased him was the coarse and simple one."[136]

Not to mention the great personalities of the early period of Islam, nor even 'Umar ibn 'Abd al-Aziz, who was a rightly- guided caliph, we refer here only to personalities of much lower stature when compared with men of the above-mentioned genre. Among the humble followers of the Holy Prophet, one comes across, among others, great rulers whose self-denial, detachment, piety and scrupulousness, absolute indifference to worldly life, its vanities and its false glories constitute man's pride and have left an indelible impress on history. Nüruddin Zangi, Salahuddin Ayyübi[137], Nāsiruddin Mahmood, Muzaffar Halimand Aurangzeb Alamgir: the lives of all these are excellent examples of indifference to the world and of self-denial. Even during the lifetime of the Mirzā, there were numerous God-loving persons who had no love for worldly riches, and who distributed every cent of what they received among the poor and the needy. The more people turned towards these men, and

---

[136] Sifat al- Safwah, Vol. I.p. 122.

[137] The biographer of the Sultan and his close confidant Qadi Ibn Shaddad writes: "The Sultan had left only 47 dirhams as his inheritance! He left no estates, no house, no property, garden, village or cultivated area. In his burial, not even a cent was spent from his legacy, all was brought on loan, including even the grassloads for the grave. The arrangement for burial was made by his Minister Qazi Fädil by some permissible and legitimate means". And he was the sovereign of Syria, Egypt, the Sudan, Iraq, Hijaz and almost the whole area that is now known as the Middle East. (*Al-Nawadir-i- Sultānia*, p. 6).

the more they received by way of gifts from people, the greater was their detachment from these riches. In the lifetime of the Mirzā we find such illustrious men of God as Maulana Fazlur Rahmän Ganj Muradābādı, Maulānā Rashid Ahmad Gangohi, Maulānā Syed Abdullah Ghaznavi, Maulānā Muhammad Naim Frangi Mahli who were admirable examples of Muslim piety and austerity.[138]

A Sign of Prophethood

Thus, a pure, self-denying life, whose character remains unruffled by vicissitudes of poverty and wealth was not unknown to the Mirzā. In fact, he reckoned it to be a proof of the truth of the Holy Prophet's prophethood. He wrote:

> "And when after a long time, Islam became supreme he (i.e. the Holy Prophet) did not accumulate any treasure for self-enrichment and self-glorification; nor did he erect any building or monument; nor did he devise means for a life of royal ease or luxury; nor did he seize any other opportunity for personal benefit. Whatever came was all spent on taking care of the orphans and the poor, on the widows and on those in debt; as for himself, he ate not even once to his full satisfaction."[139]

Religious Teacher or Political Leader

Now, let us attempt to study the Mirza's life according to the above-mentioned standard which he himself recognizes as a criterion of piety. What we note in regard to the Mirzā, how- ever, is

---

[138] See an account of their lives in Nuzhat ul- Khawatir, Vol. VIII.

[139] Barahin- i- Ahmadiyah, Vol. I, p. 117.

the marked change in the two phases of his life, his earlier life of anonymity and poverty, and the latter phase, when he was adored by his followers and received lavish presentations from them. Instead of finding in his conduct any resemblance to the saintly and angelic lives of the religious personalities of Islam, we find his life resembling that of world-seeking political leaders or founders of non-religious movements. In the last phase of his life (when a man is conscious that the time of his reckoning and meeting with God is close) we find him rolling in prosperity and luxury in a manner which reminds us of political careerists rather than of sincere servants of the cause of God. This question assumed such importance that it caused uneasiness among his sincere and close followers, some of whom were, in the end, forced to give vent to their feelings of uneasiness and disgust.

Family Life of the Mirzā

Among the followers, Khwājā Kamaluddin was particularly suspicious and discontented with the luxurious way in which the Mirza's family lived. He mentioned to his friends that the ladies of his own family who had observed the luxurious life and the high standard of living of the Mirza's family were not prepared at all to make sacrifices and remain content with a simple, austere life in order to save money for the cause of the movement. Once he told Maulavi Muhammad Ali (a former Amir of the Jamaat-i-Ahmadiyah, Lahore), and Maulavi Sarwar Shāh Qādiyānī, a noted scholar of the Qādiānı movement:

"I have a question for which I have no answer. Please provide me with one. Formerly we used to tell our ladies that we should live the lives of the Companions who ate meagre and coarse food and wore rough dress and gave away whatever they could save to the cause of God. We urged them to do the same. By means of the admoni- tions, we used to save some money and send it to Qâdian. But when our ladies themselves went to Qādiān and came to know of the actual situation by living there, they defiantly came to us and told us that we were liars. They said that they had seen the manner in which the lives of the Prophets and Companions were being lived in Qādiān! Not even a fraction of the comfort and luxury enjoyed by the women there is available to those outside (Qādiān) although their money is of their own earning while the money used by them (i.e. in Qadıān) is that which is for national purposes and is national money. Hence, they said, we were liars who had been deceiving them and that they would never again be deceived by us. Hence, they refuse to give us any money to be sent to Qādiān."

Khwājā Kamaluddin also added: "There is a favourite reply which you give to the people. This cannot hold in my case, for I know things personally."[140]

Objections relating to Financial Matters

It seems that the public kitchen which was in the charge of the Mirzā himself had caused grave doubts in the minds of many of his sincere followers. This controversy went quite far. Among those who protested the most important was Khwājā Kamaluddin. Maulavi Muhammad Ali supported him. On one occasion the Khwājā told Maulavi Mohammad 'Alı:

"What a shame. You are aware how arduously the money of the people is collected, and then this money is not spent for the

[140] Kashf al-Ikhtilaf, p. 13 (cited in Qadiani Mazhab)

national purposes for which people donate it after slashing off their expenditures even on their bare necessities. Instead, the money is spent to gratify personal desires. And then, the amount of money too is quite large. It is so large that only if the money specified for public kitchen was managed properly, it alone would be sufficient to meet the requirements of those projects which were started and then have been lying in suspense for want of funds."[141]

These objections also reached the ears of the Mirzā and he felt greatly incensed. Maulavi Sarwar Shah writes the following:

"I have reliably come to know that the Promised Messiah (upon him be the salutations and peace of God) has expressed great sorrow that despite his declaration that it is the desire of God that the management of the public kitchen remained in his hands, and that if anything else were to happen the public kitchen would come to an end, yet persons like the Khwājā are such that they constantly ask him to entrust the management of the kitchen to them and have invidious doubts about him."[142]

Before his death, the Mirzā referred with grief to the accusations of misappropriation of funds. In a letter to Maulavi Hakim Nūruddin, Mirzā Bashiruddin writes:

"The Hazrat (i.e. Mirza Ghulam Ahmad) said shortly before his (fatal) illness that the Khwājā (Kamaluddin) and Maualvi Muhammad Ali, etc., cast aspersions about him that he had misappropriated national fund. They should not do so, (he said) or else it would not have good consequences for them. He said that the Khwājā had brought a letter from Maulavi Muhammad Ali the same

---

[141] Ibid., p. 15.

[142] Kashf al- Ikhtalāj, p. 14

day. He added that Maulavi Muhammad 'Ali wrote that the expenditure on the kitchen was quite meagre and asked what happened to the rest of the thousands of rupees which had been received. When he came home, he expressed great anger and said: 'These people consider us to be mis appropriators. What do these people have to do with this money? If I were to disassociate myself all income would cease.' Then (on another occasion) when a deputation had gone to collect funds for construction works, the Khwājā said to Maulavi Muhammad Ali: 'The Hazrat (Mirzā) himself lives a life of great comfort and luxury and teaches us to donate by reducing our expenses. To this, Maulavi Muhammad Ali replied that although this could not be denied, this was an element of human shortcoming in him; and now, why should it be essential for us to follow this element of human shortcoming in the Prophet."[143]

A novel Sources of Income

One of the biggest sources of income was the sale of a title to burial in the "heavenly graveyard" at Qadian. This had been instituted by the Mirzā himself, who had ingenuously laid down the terms and conditions for buying the title to burial there. The high price of this title, as well as the temptation-provoking manner of announcement,[144] conjures up in one's mind the memories of the sale of indulgences by the Catholic Church during the Middle Ages. This, however, gave the Qādiānı headquarters a permanent and large

[143] Letter of Mirzā Bashiruddin Mahmood to Maulavi Hakim Ntūruddin, the first Khalifah of the Mirzā, in Haqiqat-al-Ikhtilaf, by Maulavi Muhammad 'Alī, p. 50. On this subject, we have confined ourselves to the statements of the closest confidants of the Mirzā, otherwise, there is a good deal of material worth studying in such books as al-Zikr al-Hakim by Dr. Abdul Hakim.

[144] For details, see the Mirza's treatise *al-Wasiyat*, pp. 11-23.

source of income. This, in fact, developed into one of the most important departments of the Qādiāni movement. Al-Fadhl, the official Qadiani mouthpiece has aptly observed: "The 'heavenly graveyard' is such a central point of this movement and an institution or department of such dimensions that it excels in importance all other departments."[145]

What has all this led to? Qādiān before the partition, and now Rabwah, its successor in Pakistan, developed into a quasi-religious state. In this state, the "Prophetic family" of Qadian, and its head, Mirzā Bashiruddin Mahmood[146], enjoy all the appurtenances of governmental power, all the authority which is vested in a religious dictator and a despotic ruler and all those opportunities of self-indulgence which are available to the most wealthy and powerful men of today. The inner life of this "spiritual and religious centre" and the moral character of its head remind one of Hassan ibn Sabbah and his Fort of al- Mūt, which was a mysterious centre of religious despotism and licentious self-indulgence in the fifth century of Hijrah.[147]

---

[145] *al-Fadhl*, Vol. XXIV, No. 65, dated September 15, 1936.

[146] This was written when Mirzā Bashiruddin Mahmood was alive and was head of the Qādiāni movement.

[147] For details see Rahat Malik, Dawr- i- Hazir kā Mahabi Amir.

2: Seedling of the British

Great Britain and the Islamic World

In the early part of the nineteenth century, the onslaught of European powers on the world of Islam had already started, and their authority and influence had spread to several Muslim countries. In this eastward expansion of European nations, Britain was in the forefront. She was in the vanguard of the military advance, as well as economic and political predominance over Eastern countries. India and Egypt were already under her occupation. Ottoman Turkey was one of the main fields of British diplomatic operations and conspiracies. Her political ambitions also menaced the Arabian Peninsula.

In India, the British domination had virtually been established even before 1857. The successors of Shah Jahan and Aurangzeb had become idle pensioners of the British, and were paralysed politically. The reins of power in the sub-continent were in the hands of the British. In 1799, the gallant career of Tipū Sultan came to an end with his martyrdom, and the way was paved for further British penetration. Being confident of the stability of the British power in India, the Christian missionaries had launched upon their proselytising endeavours.

The first targets of these missions were, naturally, the Muslims from whom the British had snatched their political power. The principles of Islam began to be ridiculed. The country was led to social breakdown and moral anarchy. The Islamic bases of social life were shaken. Western civilization began to make inroads into the homes of Muslims and into their hearts and minds. Atheism began to catch the imagination of educated young men and developed almost as a fad.

The reaction against all these led to the famous Indian struggle for independence of 1857 which, as it is well known, was led by the Muslims. The British emerged as the triumphant power and India became part of the imperial domains of the British Crown. The infuriated victors took their revenge to the full upon the rebellious Muslims, who were responsible for the "Mutiny". The British launched on a policy to systematically humiliate them. They hanged many members of the aristocracy and quite a few ulama. They confiscated their *awqaf* (religious endowments), closed on them the avenues of respectable employment and completely weeded them out of the country's administration.[148] Thus, the Muslims had become members of a humiliated and vanquished nation. Their situation reflected the eternal reality embodied in this Quranic verse:

"Kings, when they enter a country, despoil it, and make the noblest of it meanest." (27:34)

In this country, the position of the British was not merely that of ungodly and tyrannical rulers. They also represented a culture which became the mainspring of atheism, moral cynicism, and social anarchy in the country. In practice, they were opposed to all those values, religious and moral standards, on which the Islamic way of life rests. They were a criminal nation whose history was replete with wrongs perpetrated against the world of Islam:

---

[148] Details are given in W. W. Hunter's Our Indian Mussalmans and Sir Sayyid Ahmad's *Asbab-i-Baghawat-i-Hind*.

The attitude of Prophets

Now, if we were to consult the records of the prophets and their true successors and sincere followers, they clearly indicate that they have always opposed and resisted tyrants and wrong- doers and have abstained from whatever might support or strengthen such despots. The following statement of Moses (upon him be the peace of God) found in the Holy Qur'an is significant :

"O my Lord! For that Thou hast bestowed Thy grace on me never shall I be a help to those who Sin." (28:17)

The resentment that he had against unbelief and tyranny, and their standard bearers, is also borne out by the following prayer, which he made to God in respect of Pharaoh and his courtiers:

"Our Lord! Thou hast indeed bestowed on Pharaoh and his chiefs splendour and wealth in the life of the Present, and so, Our Lord, they mislead (men) from Thy path. Deface, Our Lord, the features of their wealth, and send hardness to their hearts, so that they will not Believe until they see the grievous penalty." (10:88)

God Himself instructs the believers to adopt the following attitude with regard to tyrants and oppressors:

"And incline not to those who do wrong, or the Fire will seize you; and ye have no protectors other than God; nor shall ye be helped." (11: 113)

Then there is a well-known Tradition:

"The best (kind of) *jihad* is (to proclaim) the word of Truth in the face of a tyrannical ruler."

The Holy Prophet, his noble Companions, and his true successors never cooperated with any power which stood for falsehood and injustice. Their tongues were never soiled with praises and eulogies of tyrants. The history of Islam is replete with courageous expressions of protest and revolt against oppressors. There is no period in Islamic history, and no area of the Muslim world, which has not witnessed this noble struggle.

Protagonist of the British Imperialism

But contrary to the illustrious teachings of the Holy Qur'an and the spirit of Islam and in violation of the noble example of the Prophets, their companions and their followers, Mirza Ghulam Ahmad, who claimed to be a God-sent messenger, is full of praise for the greatest force of evil of his age-the British Government. He never tires of praising that very government which had been the usurper of Islamic dominions, the greatest rival to the temporal power of Islam, and a great standard-bearer of atheism and moral degeneration. He praises the British with a vehemence which casts doubt on the motives of any conscientious man, not to say of a prophet. From the very beginning he was so greatly concerned with praising the British that there is hardly any work of his which has remained immune from flattery. We have already noted that in his first book, *Barahin-i-Ahmadiyah* (vol. I), he had lavishly praised the British, had recounted their benevolent achievements and services, had assured them of Muslim loyalty, and had expressed his views against the doctrine of jihad. These trends persisted in his writings right up to the end of his life. He almost produced a whole library of books on the subject. In these books he returned again and again to assuring the British of his unswerving loyalty and recounted the services of his family to the British along with his own support. At a time when the feeling of Islamic self-respect was in need of being aroused and the nation needed the impulse to resist its oppressors, he again and again repeated that jihad had become out-of-date. Below are a few excerpts from the Mirza's own writings to illustrate his trend of thought:

"The greater part of my life has been spent supporting and defending the British Government. And I have written so many books regarding the prohibition of jihad and obedience to the British that were they to be gathered together, they would fill fifty bookcases. Such books have been disseminated over all the countries: Arabia, Egypt, Syria, Kabul, and Rüm. I have always endeavoured that Muslims became true well-wishers of this Government, and their hearts were purged of baseless traditions about the bloody Mahdi and the bloody Messiah and those fanatical teachings which corrupt the hearts of the stupid."[149]

At another place, he propounds allegiance to the British as one of the two pillars of faith:

"My religion, which I have been explaining again and again, is that there are two parts of Islam: one, to obey the exalted Allah, and second, to obey the government which has established peace, and has provided its shadow of protection as against oppression. Such a government is the British Government."[150]

In a request to the Lieutenant Governor of Punjab on 24th February 1898, he wrote: -

"The other thing worth mentioning is that from my early age till now when I am about sixty years of age, I have been engaged, with my pen and tongue, in an important task to turn the hearts of Muslims towards the true love and good-will and sympathy for the

---

[149] Tiryaq al- Qulb, p. 15.

[150] "Ishtihar Government Ki Tawajjuh ke Lai'q" in Shahadat al- Qur'an, p. 3.

British Government, and to obliterate the idea of jihad from the hearts of the less wise among them, since it stands in the way of cordiality and a sincere mutual relationship. And I notice that my writings have had a tremendous influence on the hearts of Muslims and hundreds of thousands of people have changed."[151]

At another place, he observes:

"I have written scores of books in Arabic, Persian and Urdu with the view that jihad against the benevolent government was in no way justified; rather, wholehearted obedience to it was a religious duty. I had these books published at great cost and then had them distributed in Islamic countries. And I know that these books had a great influence even in this country. The people who owe allegiance to me are growing into a party whose hearts are filled to the brim with sincere fidélity to the Government whose moral condition is excellent; I think they will be a boon to this country for they are wholeheartedly ready to sacrifice themselves for the government."[152]

At yet another place, he wrote:

"The service which has been rendered for the sake of the British Government was that I published and distributed in this country and other Islamic countries about fifty thousand books, treatises and leaflets, stating that the British Government is the benefactor of Muslims and therefore it should be the duty of every Muslim to obey it sincerely and heartily feel grateful to it and to pray for it. And, I had these books published in different languages, that

---

[151] *Tabligh- i- Risalat*, Vol. VII, p. 10.

[152] *Arizah Badli- i- Khidmat* Government *'Aliyah Angrezi min jānib Mirzā Ghulām Ahmad Qadiani Saheb*, cited in Mir Qasim Ali Qadiani's *Tabligh- i- Risalat*, Vol. VI, p. 65.

is, Urdu, Persian and Arabic, and then distributed them in all the countries of Islam, so much so that I had them distributed even in the two holy cities of Islam, Mecca and Medina, and, as far as possible, also, in the capital of Rüm- Constantinople, and Syria, Egypt and Kabul and many other cities of Afghanistan. The result was that hundreds of thousands of people gave up their filthily ideas about jihad, which had permeated their hearts due to the teachings of ignorant mullās. I am proud of this service which I have been able to render, and no Muslim of British India can boast of a parallel record."[153]

Abrogation of Jihad

The Mirza's main concern was jihad which, indeed, had caused the greatest worry to the British not only in India but in all Muslim countries (quite a number of which had already been occupied by the British). The Mirza proclaimed jihad to have been abrogated for ever and put forward this as the sign of his being the Promised Messiah. He proclaimed:

"Thirdly, the clock which will be installed in some part of the wall of this minaret, would signify that the people should realise that the time for the opening of the doors of the heavens has arrived. From now on there shall be no terrestrial jihad and wars shall cease. It has been mentioned earlier in the Traditions that when the Messiah would come, wars for the sake of religion would be prohibited. From now on whosoever shall raise the sword for the sake of religion and slay the infidels by proclaiming himself to be a ghazı, he will be a disobedient rebel of God and His Prophet. Open Sahih al-Bukhari and read the hadith about the promised Messiah,

---

[153] *Sitara- i- Kaiseriah*. p. 3.

that is, the one in which there occurs the expression which means that when the Messiah will come jihad would cease. Now the Messiah has come, and it is he who is speaking to you.[154]

He regards this abrogation of jihad as the greatest object of his advent:

To cite his own words:

"In short, I have not come in order to stimulate war and strife. I have appeared in order to open, in the manner of the first Messiah, the doors of peace. If the foundation of peace is not amidst us, then our whole religious order is useless, and it is also meaningless to believe in it.[155]

At another place, he becomes even more explicit:

"I believe that as my followers increase, the believers in the doctrine of jihad will decrease. For, accepting me to be the Messiah and Mahdi itself means the rejection of the doctrine of *jihad*."[156]

Citadel of the British Government

In his Arabic treatise Nurul-Haq he went as far as to say that he was the citadel and amulet for protecting the British Government:

"I am entitled to assert that I am unique in respect of these services. And I am entitled to say that I am an amulet and a citadel to protect it from afflictions. My Lord has given me glad tidings and has said that He will not chastise them as long as I am among them.

---

[154] *Khutba- i- Ilhamiyalı.* Appendix entitled Ishtihar Chandah Minäratal Masih.

[155] *Tiryāqal- Qulub*, p. 335.

[156] *Tabligh- i- Risalat*, Vol. VII. p. 17.

So, the Government has no parallel and equal to me in supporting and assisting it and the Government shall know this if it is capable of knowing people."[157]

Seedling of the British

In an application submitted to the Lieutenant-Governor of Punjab on 24th February 1898, he wrote:

"I have to submit that in regard to a family which has proven itself to be loyal; had ever been prepared to make sacrifices for the Government during the last fifty years; of which the respectable officials of the exalted Government have borne weighty testimonies in their official letters about its being all long a well-wisher and servant of the British Government; which is the self-implanted seedling (of loyalty), the Government should exercise utmost caution and make all possible efforts to know about it and pay attention to it. The Government should also instruct its lower officials that they should look towards me and my group with the eyes of kindness and benevolence in view of the established loyalty and sincerity of this family."[158]

In another application he refers to himself and his group as 'those who had been brought up as tried and true friends of the British those who had earned a good name with the Government and had enjoyed its merciful kindness.'

Cause of opposition to Missionaries

The Mirza was possessed of such a profound feeling of loyalty for the British that he used to adopt numerous measures in order to

---

[157] *Nur al- Haq*, p. 34.

[158] *Tabligh- i- Risalat*, Vol. VII, p. 19.

assuage the deep hatred and resentment of Muslims against the British. His enthusiastic opposition to the Christian missionaries, according to his own view, was also motivated by the same desire. The efforts of these missionaries to repudiate Islam and to slander the Holy Prophet, according to the Mirzā, had infuriated the Muslims and was likely to prove detrimental to the interests of the British Government. Hence, he showed great zeal, out of expediency and with deliberation, in order that the popular Muslim fury might abate, and they might somewhat calm down. He writes:

> "I also confess that when some of the writings of priests and Christian missionaries became extremely severe and exceeded moderation, and especially when very filthy writings began to appear in Nür Afshan, a Christian paper from Ludhiana, and when these writers used, God forbid, derisive language with regard to our Prophet (upon him be the peace and benediction of Allah), I feared that in the hearts of Muslims, who are a sentimental people, these words might have a highly provocative effect. In order to subdue their indignation, I thought that the proper policy would be to write rejoinders to these writings in a somewhat harsh manner so that the towering anger of these easily- inflammable people could be suppressed and no breach of peace in the country might take place."[159]

Spies of the British

The impact of these teachings, propagated with religious sanctions, was that loyalty to the British and zeal to serve it, became

---

[159] Tiryaq al-Qulub. Appendix 3, p. 31 entitled "A Humble Request to the Exalted Government."

an integral part of the Qadiani outlook and character. It is not surprising that the British Government found from among them quite a few who sincerely and loyally served the cause of the British and did not hesitate even to shed their blood for them. In Afghanistan, there was an enthusiastic Qādiāni preacher by the name of 'Abdul Latif. The main task that he had undertaken was to purge the Afghans of that spirit of jihad because of which the Afghans had never tolerated the rule of any non-Muslim power over their land, and which had always been a source of headache to the British. It was due to this kind of preaching that the Afghan Government executed him. Mirzā Bashiruddin Mahmood has mentioned this on the authority of an Italian author. He says:

"The Italian author writes that Sahibzādā 'Abdul Latif was martyred because he preached against jihad and the Afghans had begun to fear that the spirit of freedom of the Afghans would weaken and the British would predominate."[160]

He adds:

Had our people in Afghanistan remained silent and refrained from explaining the Ahmadī viewpoint in respect of jihad, they would not have been blameworthy from the viewpoint of the Shariat. But they fell victims of the excessive zeal they had for the British Government, they courted punishment because of the sympathy for it which they had imbibed at Qadiān.[161]

In the same way, certain papers and letters were found with Mulla Abdul Hakim and Mulla Nūr Ali Qadiani which proved that they were disloyal to the Afghan government and were agents and

---

[160] al- Fadhl, August 6, 1925.

[161] Ibid.

spies of the British. Al-Fadhl, the Qadiani mouthpiece, published this piece of news from Aman-i-Afghan:

"The Minister for Home Affairs of the Afghan Government has published the following announcement:

"Two persons of Kabul, Mullā 'Abdul Hakim Chahār Asia'1 and Mulla Nur Ali, a shopkeeper, had become enamoured of Qadiani beliefs and used to mislead people from the right path by preaching that creed. The people who were angered at this filed a suit against them. The result was that these persons having been proved guilty were transported at the hands of the people to the realm of non-existence on Thursday, Rajab 11. Against them there had also been pending a suit for long, and letters of foreigners of a conspiratorial nature and harmful to the interests of the Afghan kingdom had been captured which proved that they had sold themselves to the enemies of Afghanistan."[162]

In his address of welcome to the Prince of Wales on January 19, 1922, Mirzā Bashiruddin Mahmood proudly mentions all these incidents, making it clear that all these sacrifices were because of their loyalty to the British.[163]

Miscalculation

Looking at the power, consolidation and extent of the British Empire, the Mirzā believed that the British power in India would remain for ever. Hence, tying up their own fate with that of the British Empire, and identifying their own future with the future of the British seemed very wise and an act of great political far-

---

[162] Al- fadhl, March 3, 1925.

[163] A Present to His Royal Highness the Prince of Wales. pp. 7-8.

sightedness. And, indeed, from someone who is shorn of deep religious and political insight such a conclusion was not strange. It was impossible for the Mirzā to foresee that not even half a century would pass after his death when the seemingly unshakable power of the British would be shaken and the power which he considered to be "the shadow of God" and "refuge of religion" would leave India, lock, stock and barrel, and, not only that, but it would also collapse the world over.

The servile manner in which the Mirzā has given expression of his loyalty to this un-Islamic, indeed, anti-Islamic power, and the zeal he has shown in preaching to the Muslims that they ought to relish their state of political enslavement as a boon, is unbecoming of the position which he claims for himself. Iqbal has stressed this contradiction in some of his verses which say:

The Sheikh is a murid of the Firangi Lord,
Speaks he, though, from the heights of Bayazid.
He said: Religion's glory lies in slavery.
And life consists of the lack of ego (*khudi*).
He reckoned the state of others to be a blessing.
Danced around the cathedral and fell down dead.[164]

[164] Pa Cho Büved hard as *Aqwam- i- Sharq*.

3: Prophet as Mudslinger

Soft-spokenness of the Prophets

The Prophets of God and their pious followers have always been known for their graceful and decent mode of expression, patience and calm endurance, large-heartedness and magnanimity. Benevolent even to their enemies, they returned good wishes for abuses; benediction for curses; humility for insolence; and temperance and gracefulness for niggardly meanness. Their tongues were never soiled with abusive and filthy language. To sting people by harsh satires and invidious sarcasms, to scoff and jeer at the people, to pinch them by vulgar attacks - all these are far too low to be found in their noble lives. If they were ever forced to refute or denounce someone, they did so in clear, simple terms. They never stooped to adopt abject methods such as attacking the opponent's birth, denigrating his lineage, or ridiculing him in the manner of a court-jester. Their expressions, whether they were in favour of someone or against him, bear the mark of the decency and elegance of their natures, and the nobility of their minds. The Companions have left the following account of the Holy Prophet Mohammad's discourse:

"The Messenger of Allah-upon him be the peace and blessings of Allah-was neither harsh-tongued by nature nor by will, nor did he ever indulge in undignified talk in market-places."[165]

The Prophet himself laid down the norm of speech for the believers:

---

[165] Tirmidhi.

"The believer is not wont to attacking or cursing people nor does he use harsh and filthy expressions."[166]

On the contrary, according to the Prophet, the characteristic of a hypocrite (*munafiq*) is that "whenever he quarrels, he resorts to abuses."[167]

The Mirzā himself admits that those who have been endowed with religious and spiritual leadership ought to be possessed of forbearance and self-control, forgiveness and patience. He writes:

"Since the Imāms encounter all kinds of wicked, lowly and filthy-tongued people, they have to have a moral calibre of the highest order so that they might not be stirred by egotistic anger or fanaticism and thus people are not deprived of their blessings. It is a matter of great shame that someone is called "the friend of God" yet he remains afflicted with base morals and is incapable of bearing obloquy with composure. As for a man who is called the spiritual leader of his age (*Imām-i-Zaman*), if he is so thin-skinned that even the least provocative remark sends him into a fit of rage, such a person can in no way be considered the Imam of his age."[168]

But contrary to the expectations raised by these words, the manner in which the Mirzā has dealt with his critics - and these included some of the most respected religious scholars and spiritual leaders-brings him out as a person who lacked even the most elementary sense of decency and decorum. "Offsprings of harlots"

---

[166] Tirmidhi.

[167] Bukhari and Muslim.

[168] Zururat al- Imām, p. 8.

seems to have been one of the favourite nicknames which he very often gave to his opponents.[169]

The 'best' specimens of his abuses are found in his Arabic writings-prose as well as poetry. Here are a few of them.

"Now, since these people abuse me, I have already taken off all their clothes and have reduced them to unrecognisable carcases."[170]

"These enemies have become the swine of our wilderness, and their women are even worse than bitches."[171]

An Arabic poem indited by the Mirzā to denounce one of his opponents; Maulvi Sa'ad Ullah of Ludhiana, is much too unseemly to be reproduced here.[172]

For such illustrious religious personages of his time as Maulana Muhammad Husain Batālawi, Maulānā Sayyed Nazir Husain Muhaddith Dehlawi, Maulānā Abdul Haq Haqqāni, Mufti Abdullah Tonkwi, Maulānā Ahmad 'Alī Saharanpūri, Maulānā Ahmad Hasan Amorhi, and Hazrat Maulānā Rashid Ahmad Gangohi, he used invectives, such as, 'wolves and dogs', 'accursed satan', 'blind devil', 'the gang of abducters', 'the doomed', and the 'accursed' etc."[173] In the same way, he composed a satirical poem about the well-known scholar and spiritual leader of his time, Pir Mihr Ali Shah of Golra. A few of its couplets reads:

---

[169] See for example. Ana-i-Kemätät-i-Islam, p. 547. Nür al-Haq, Vol. I p 123. Anjām-i-Atham, p. 282, etc.

[170] *Anjam- i- Atham*, p. 158.

[171] *Najm al- Hudā*, p. 15.

[172] Ibid., pp. 281-82,

[173] *Ijāz- i- Ahmadi*, pp. 75-76.

"So, I said: O Land of Golra, upon thee be curse. Thou hast been accursed because of the accursed ones; and thy abode shall be the place of torment.

"This petty man, like lowly people has addressed me in abusive terms. Every man is tested in the time of hostility."[174]

These abuses were often not enough to gratify him. On such occasions he would not merely curse his opponents but write the word 'curse' with regard to them a certain number of times. For instance, with regard to Maulānā Thana Ullah Amritsarī, he wrote the word 'accurst' ten times consecutively. In regard to Christians, he wrote this word one thousand times.[175] This, indeed, makes a queer reflection on his nature.

We would close this section by reproducing just a few more examples of the Mirza's vituperations against his opponents. Addressing the 'ulama, he wrote:

"O debased class of Maulavis. How long will you conceal the truth? When will the time come for you to give up your Jewish habits? O tyrant Maulavīs, pity be on you, that you made the cattle-like common folk drink from the same cup of falsehood of which you had drunk."[176]

He also wrote:

"Of all animals, the filthiest and most repellent is pig. But filthier than pigs are those who, owing to their base desires, conceal the testimony of truth. O corpse-eating Maulavīs! O filthy spirits!

---

[174] See the long letter of the Mirzā in Arabic in *Anjām-i-Atham*, pp. 251-52.

[175] See Nur al- Haq. pp. 100-1 121-2

[176] Anjam- i- Atham, p. 21

Pity be on you for you have concealed the true evidence of Islam out of hostility. O worms of darkness! How can you hide the radiant rays of truth?"[177]

"Will these people be prepared to swear? No, never. For they are liars and are eating the carcass of falsehood like dogs."[178]

This subject is neither pleasant for the author, nor palatable for the readers. We, therefore, close the chapter, leaving it for the readers to guess the bloom of the Mirzā's spring on the basis of the few flowers of his garden we have presented here as specimens.

---

[177] Ibid.

[178] Ibid., p. 25 n.

4: An Unfulfilled Prophecy

In 1888, when the Mirzā was fifty years old, he asked one of his relatives, Mirzā Ahmad Beg for the hand of his young daughter Muhammadı Begum. The Mirzā made it clear that he had been commissioned by God for that task and God had promised him, in unequivocal terms, and that this marriage would, therefore, certainly take place.

In a leaflet which was distributed on July 10, 1888, the Mirzā wrote:

"The Omnipotent and Omniscient God has asked me that I should seek the hand of the elder daughter of this man (Ahmad Beg); should tell him that good conduct and courtesy to be shown to him would depend on this (i.e. his acceptance of the marriage proposal); her marriage with me would be a source of blessing and a sign of mercy for her father; and that he would have his share in all those blessings and mercies which have been laid down in the leaflet dated February 20, 1886 but if he declines to marry her, then the girl would meet an extremely tragic end. The other person to whom she would be married would die within two and a half years after the day of wedding, and so would die the father of the girl within three years, and her household would be afflicted with discord and poverty and adversity, and during the intervening period the girl would encounter several events of unpleasant and grievous nature."[179]

In his work, *Izala-i-Awhām*, he mentions this prophecy in the following manner:

---

[179] This announcement has been reproduced in full by the *Mirzā in Ainā- i-Kamalat-i-Isam*, p 286. It has also been reproduced by Qasim 'Ali Ahmadi in *Tabligh-i-Risalat*, Vol. I, pp. 111-18.

"By way of prophecy, the Exalted God revealed it to this humble one that ultimately the elder daughter of Mirzā Ahmad Beg, son of Mirzā Gāmān Beg Hoshiārpūrī, would be married to me. These people would resort to great hostility and would place obstacles in the way, but in the end, it would surely take place. The Exalted God would, by all possible means, bring her to me, whether as a virgin or a widow, and would remove all impediments, and would, of necessity, fulfil this task, and none would be able to prevent it."[180]

Significance of the Prophecy

This problem related to the family life of the Mirzā and normally, such problems should be of little interest to a historian. There are millions of people who strive for the hand of the girl of their choice. Some of them succeed, others do not. But the endeavour of the Mirzā to marry this particular girl is a case of uncommon significance, in so far as the Mirzā put it forth as the criterion of judging the veracity of his claim to prophethood. After mentioning his prophecy that he would ultimately marry the said girl, he said: "This should be clear to the people that there can be no better criterion of testing our truth or falsehood than our prophecy."[181]

One might perhaps be inclined to think that misunderstandings in respect of the messages from the unseen world are possible, for, sometimes people misinterpret these messages by mixing up the words of inspiration. In respect of this prophecy of the Mirzā, however, there is no question of any such

[180] *Izala- i- Awham*, p. 198.

[181] *Ainä- i- Kamālāt- i- Islām*, p. 288.

possibility. The challenging tone of the prophecy rules out all such possibilities. In his own words:

"The prophecies which are presented before opponents for the purpose of vindicating some claim, contain a peculiar kind of light and guidance since the inspired ones, who, by concentrating their attention on God, generally succeed in having a clear concept of their meaning and nature."[182]

It is also possible that some people might not attach much importance to this prophecy of the Mirzā, because of his habit of making prophecies all too frequently. It is true that his writings are replete with prophecies. This particular prophecy, however, has a uniqueness of its own in so far as the Mirzā put if forward as a heavenly sign and as a verdict in his favour. He not only made this prophecy the criterion of his own truth and falsehood, but also of the victory or defeat of Islam. On July 10, 1888, he announced:

"Then, when I repeatedly meditated in order to seek clarification and elaboration of the prophecy, it was made known to me that God has pre-determined that the elder daughter of the addressee (i.e. Mirza Ahmad Beg) will ultimately be married to this humble one (after all impediments had been removed) and this event will make the irreligious people (true) Muslims, and provide guidance to the misguided."[183]

The original inspiration in Arabic in this connection, when translated into English, reads:

"They falsified our signs, and they had been laughing at them for long. So, God will be your helper in dealing with those who are

---

[182] *Izala- i- Awhām*, p. 202.

[183] *Aina- i- Kamālai- i- Islām*, p. 286, and *Tabligh- i- Risālal*, Vol. I, p. 116.

obstructing this task and, in the end, they will bring this girl to you. There is none who can put off the words of God. Your God is Omnipotent, so that whatever happens, takes place by His will. You are with Me, and I am with you; and you shall shortly reach the stage whereat you shall be praised. This means that even though the stupid and ignorant people indulge in vilification and utter unbecoming words for you, out of their inner corruption and invidious understanding, but they will ultimately feel ashamed after they have witnessed the succour of God and, as a result of the manifestation of truth, there will be praise for you all round."[184]

It was still possible for people to forget the matter. But the Mirzā was so confident about the fulfilment of this prophecy that he kept on reiterating it in an increasingly forceful and confident manner. He said:

"Wait for (the fulfilment of) the prophecy mentioned in the announcement of July 10, 1888, along with which there is also appended the inspiration: And they ask thee if this is true. Say: Yes, by my Lord, it is true, and you cannot prevent it from taking place. We have Ourselves wed thee to her. There is none to change My words. And on seeing the sign, they will turn their faces aside and will say: This is a thorough deception, and a thorough magic.[185]

In his letter addressed to the 'ulamu and spiritual mentors India in Arabic, the Mirzā said:

"Predestination is bound to prevail and God has finally decreed it, and so the time for it (i.e. marriage) will inevitably come. By the One who has sent to us Muhammad al- Mustafa and made him

---

[184] *Aina- i- kamältä- i- Islām*, p. 286; *Tabligh- i- Risalat*, Vol. I, p. 116.

[185] Asmani Faisla, p. 40.

the best of messengers and the best of creatures, verily this is truth, and you will see it, and I shall make this news the criterion of my truth and false- hood. And I did not say this until I was informed about it from God.[186]

Emphasising the significance of this prophecy and stressing it to be the sign of God, he said:

"In respect of this (prophecy), some of the fair-minded Arya authors have also borne witness that if this prophecy were fulfilled, it would indeed be an act of God. And this prophecy is against a harsh people who, it seems, have drawn the sword of enmity and spite, and whosoever knows the state they are in, will be well aware of the great significance of this prophecy. Everyone who will read the announcement, no matter how prejudiced he is, is bound to agree that the content of the prophecy is beyond the capacity of man."[187]

When he felt agitated about the realization of this prophecy, owing to some serious illness which caused him the suspicion of being close to death, he received fresh inspiration to reassure him. He writes:

"Soon after this prophecy was revealed and had yet to be fulfilled (as it has not been fulfilled as yet, that is, by April 16, 1891), this humble one encountered a severe ailment bringing him so close to death that he got even his will drawn up. At that critical moment, the prophecy almost came before his eyes, and it appeared that the last moment had come and that the next day would be his day of funeral. At that time, he thought of this prophecy; that, may be, it had some other meaning which he had not understood. Then, in that

---

[186] *Anjam- i- Atham*, p. 223

[187] *Izala- i- Awhām*, p. 199.

critical condition, he received the inspiration: This thing is truth from thy Lord. Why dost thou doubt?"[188]

Thus, the Mirzā's marriage with Muhammadi Begum was a settled matter-a matter which had been decided upon in the heavens and, hence, there was no possibility of any alteration. He announced that this was not only the criterion of his veracity, but also of the veracity of the One who had communicated it to him. And since he considered himself to be the true representative and advocate of Islam, and his own prestige to be synonymous with the prestige of Islam, he regarded the matter as one involving the victory of Islam itself.

Mirzā Stoops to Conquer

But as luck would have it, Mirzā Ahmad Beg spurned the proposal and decided to give his daughter in marriage to another relative of his, Mirzā Sultan Muhammad. The Mirzā came to know of it. Owing to his exuberant enthusiasm and his intense confidence in regard to his ultimate success, the matter had already come to public knowledge. It had been mentioned in newspapers and magazines and had become an interesting topic of conversation. Hindus, Sikhs, and Muslims all were keenly interested in the developments relating to this case. The Mirza's matrimonial affair had evoked even greater interest than that of the royal families. The numerous challenges which he had published from time to time had rendered the matter even more delicate and complex. The members of the girl's family (who had religious differences with the Mirzā and whose family pride had been hurt by his public announcements), categorically rejected the Mirzā's proposal. From the Mirzā's point

[188] Ibid.

of view, however, the matter had become so serious that the establishment of matrimonial relationship had become inevitable. He had announced the prophecy in such categorical and definite terms that it was hard for him to back out of that position or to re-interpret the prophecy to mean something else than what it apparently meant.

Theoretically, however, the Mirza believed that the inspired person should strive for the fulfilment of his own prophecies and that there was nothing incompatible between this effort and his position as the recipient of an inspired prophecy.[189] It was because of this view that he himself had the eastern minaret constructed at Qadian for, it had been mentioned in the Tradition concerning the return of Jesus. Following the same principle, he set out to persuade, by all possible means, the father and other relatives of Muhammadi Begum to accept his proposal. He resorted to all the means of inducement and terrorisation which he could possibly employ. In his request as well as the announcement of July 10, 1888, both these aspects---inducement and terrorisation-are quite evident. In the event of the acceptance of the proposal of marriage he had promised Divine reward, whereas in the case of its rejection, he had threatened them with ruin.

The Mirzā also wrote letters to the relatives of Muhammadi Begum, to her father, Mirzä Ahmad Beg, to her uncle, Mirzā 'Ali Sher Beg, to her aunt, and to other relatives who could have exerted some

---

[189] He writes: "If Divine revelation makes something known as prophecy, and if it is possible that a man should fulfil it without fanning up a fitnah (evil) and resorting to illegitimate means, then making efforts for the fulfilment of such a prophecy is not only permissible, but also commendable (masnun)" *Haqiqat al-Wahi*, p. 191

influence on the decision about her marriage. He asked all these people, with great meekness and humility, to use their good offices in his favour. To Mirza Ahmad Beg (the father of the girl), he wrote:

"If you accept what I say, it will be a matter of benevolence and gratification and kindness towards me, and I will pray to the Most Compassionate One for your long life. I promise you to transfer one third of my property to your daughter, and I say honestly that I will give you whatever you will ask of me."[190]

In another letter to Mirza Ahmad Beg, he wrote:

"I still make a request to your honour, with humility and respect I have for you, not to refrain from this (marriage) relationship. For, this will be a means of great blessing for your daughter, and the Exalted Allah will open the doors of divine grace which you do not even conceive of."[191]

In a letter to Mirzā 'Alı Sher Beg, he wrote:

"If the people of your household had joined together and tried to persuade your brother, why should he not have given his consent? Do I belong to a low caste so that it would be a shame to marry the girl to me? On the other hand, he kept on seconding my proposal, but, quite recently, I have been left at the mercy of his brother, and now all have united on the question of the girl's marriage. What do I have to do with a girl? She might be married to anyone. This was merely a test: those whom I considered to be my own and from whose daughter I wanted to have offspring and my

---

[190] *Kalmah-i-Fazl-i-Rahmāni*, by Qāzi Fazl Ahmad (cited in Qādiāni Mazhab). This book is a collection of the Mirza's letters to the relatives of Muhammadi Begum. The letters are authentic and even the Mirza did not deny having written them.

[191] Ibid.

heirs are now thirsty of my blood. They are now after my honour and want me to be put to shame and to have a blackened face. It is up to God to dishonour whomsoever He wills. But so far as these people are concerned, they indeed want to hurl me into the fire."[192]

To Mirzā Ahmad, he also wrote:

"You will perhaps be aware that the prophecy of this humble one has become known to thousands of people and in my opinion, there would be perhaps more than one million people who have been informed of this prophecy...... In Lahore, I found out that thousands of Muslims fervently pray in the mosques after (congregational) prayers for the fulfilment of this prophecy."[193]

The Mirzā also came to know that 'Izzat Bibi, his own daughter-in-law (wife of his son, Mirzā Fazl Ahmad), and the mother of 'Izzat Bibi, the wife of Mirza Ali Sher Beg (who was also the aunt of Muhammadi Begum), were opposed to the Mirza's proposal and favoured the marriage of the girl to Mirzā Sultan Muhammad. This infuriated the Mirzā, and he wrote the following to 'Ali Sher Beg (the father-in-law of his son, Fazl Ahmad)

"I have already written a letter to her (i.e. to the wife of Mirzā Ali Sher Beg) that if she did not give up (pursuing) her idea and did not prevail upon her brother (i.e. Mirzā Ahmad Beg) to prevent this marriage (with Mirzā Sultan Mohammad), then, as your own intention appears to be, my son Fazl Ahmad too will not be able to keep your daughter ("Izzat Bibi) in his marriage. Rather, the very moment the wedding (of Muhammadī Begum) will take place, Fazl Ahmad will divorce your daughter. And if he does not divorce her, I

[192] *Kalma- i- Fazl- i- Rahmani*, by Qazi Fazl Ahmad (cited in Qadiani Mazhab).

[193] Ibid.

will declare him to be no longer regarded as my son and will disinherit him. But if for my sake you oppose Ahmad Beg and try to prevent him from carrying out his design, then I am at your disposal on all counts with my heart and soul. Fazl Ahmad is still obedient to me. I will convince him in every way possible and will endeavour to rehabilitate your daughter. Then whatever I have shall belong to her."[194]

The Mirzā also prevailed upon Izzat Bibi, his daughter- in-law, to write to her mother that if they did not change their mind the Mirza would have her husband divorce her and thus ruin her family life."[195]

After Muhammadi Begum's marriage, Fazl Ahmad did divorce Izzat, Bibi. Another son of the Mirzā, Sultan Ahmad, and his mother, were also of the same view as the members of. Muhammadi Begum's family. Hence, consistent with what he had said earlier, the Mirzā declared Sultan Ahmad to be no longer regarded as his son. Besides, he disinherited him and divorced his mother.[196]

However, even after the marriage of Muhammadı Begum to Mirzā Sultan Muhammad (on April 7, 1892) the Mirza did not despair. He kept on saying that ultimately the girl would become his wife. In 1901, he made the following statement under oath:

"It is true that that woman has not been married to me. But she will certainly be married to me as has been stated in the prophecy. She has been married to Sultan Muhammad; I say truly that in this court (i.e. the world) where people have laughed at

[194] *Kalma- i- Fazl- i- Rahmâni.*

[195] Ibid.

[196] In *Tabligh- i- Risal*, Vol. II, p. 9.

things which were not from me, but from God, a time will come when the events will take a strange turn and the heads of all will be downcast with remorse.

"The woman is still alive. She will inevitably come to my wedlock. I expect this to happen, rather, I have full faith in this. These are divinely ordained matters and are bound to occur."[197]

In his first announcement, the Mirzā had prophesied that the person to whom Muhammadī Begum would be married, would die within two and a half years after the marriage. This period elapsed, and Mirzā Sultan Muhammad remained alive, enjoying a happy married life. This forced the Mirzā to extend the lease of his life. In his announcement of September 6, 1896 he wrote:

"The time for divine punishment is conditionally predestined, which can be put off by fear (of God) and turning (towards God), as the whole of the Qur'an testifies. But so far as it relates to the prophecy, that is, the marriage of that woman to this humble one, that is assuredly predestined, and cannot be waived off, for, in the Divine revelation it is clearly stated that 'My words will never change'. For, if they were to change, the words of God would be false."[198]

In the same announcement, he explains another reason for the postponement of his prediction:

"The Qur'an tells us that the duration indicated in such prophecies belongs to the category of conditional predestination. Hence, owing to the appearance of factors causing some change or alteration, postponement of the stipulated term and period does

[197] Al- Hukm, August 10, 1901 (cited in Qadiani *Mazhab and Tahqiq- i- Lalbani*).

[198] *Tabligh- i- Risalat*, Vol. III, p. 115

take place. This is Divine Law, and the Qur'an is replete with this. Hence, for every prophecy which is made through inspiration or revelation, it is essential that its fulfilment should conform to the Divine Law as embodied in the Books of the Exalted God. And, at the present time, another benefit aimed at from this is that those aspects of Divine knowledge which have been lost sight of by the people should once again be manifested, and thus insight into the Qur'an should be renovated.[199]

Thus, the Mirzā insisted that his prophecy was true, and he had no doubt about its ultimate fulfilment. He again insisted that:

"I say again and again that the prophecy about the son-in-law of Ahmad Beg (i.e. Sultan Muhammad), is assuredly pre-destined. Wait for it. If I am a liar, this prophecy will not be fulfilled, and my death will come."[200]

Mirzā Sultan Muhammad had a long life. He took part in the first world war. He was wounded during the war but survived, and remained alive long after the Mirzā had died.

As for the Mirzā, he died in 1908, and his wedding, which according to him had taken place in the heavens, could not take place on the earth. In the opinion of his stauncher followers, however, nothing can as yet be said unequivocally; for, so long as human life is in existence, there is still possibility of the realisation of this prophecy. Hakim Nūruddin, the successor of the Mirzā, has given a queer explanation of the matter, but very much in tune with Qadiani casuistry. In the 'Review of Religions', he wrote the following in connection with the death of the 'Promised Messiah':

---

[199] *Tabligh- i- Risalat*, Vol. III, p. 117

[200] *Anjam- i- Athem*, p. 31n.

"Now, I would like to remind all the Muslims who have had and still have faith in the Noble Qur'an that since those addressed in it include also their offsprings, successors, and those like them, then, can this prophecy not include the daughter of Ahmad Beg, or the daughter of that daughter? Does your law of inheritance not apply the regulations regarding daughters to their daughters? And are the offsprings of the Mirzā not his agnates? I had often told dear Mian Mahmood[201] that even if the Mirzā were to die and this girl did not enter into his wedlock, my adoration of him would remain unshaken."[202]

[201] Mian Bashiruddin Mahmood, a son of the Mirza and the second head of the Qadiani movement after Hakim Nūruddin.

[202] Review of Religions, Vol. VII, no. 726, June and July, 1908, p. 279 (quoted from the Qadiani school).

PART IV:

A Critical Analysis of the Movement

1: Independent Religion and a Parallel Community

One of the illusions about Qadianism is that its emergence merely signifies the addition of one more sect to the large number of already existing sects and schools in Islam, and that the followers of Qadiānism are, at the most, a new sect. Thus, the popular impression is that Qadianism does not represent a unique phenomenon in the history of Muslim sects and juristic schools.

A careful study of Qadianism is bound to shatter this illusion and to convince every unbiased student that Qadianism is a religion by itself, and the Qadianis a separate religious community (ummah), parallel to Islam and the ummah of Islam. The following statement of the Mirzā, which has been cited by the former head of Qadiani movement, Mirzā Bashīruddin Mahmood, appears to contain no exaggeration. He said:

"The words, which came out from the lips of the Promised Messiah, keep on reverberating in my ears. He said that it was wrong that our disagreement with others lay merely on the questions of the death of the Messiah or certain other similar issues. He mentioned in detail that we differed from them in respect of the Essence of Allah, in respect of the Holy Prophet (upon him be the peace and benediction of God), in respect of the Qur'an, of prayers, of fasting, of pilgrimage, and, in short, in respect of each and every part (of religion)."[203]

---

[203] Khutba (Sermon) of Friday, al-Fadhl, July 3, 1931.

Mirzā Mahmood also affirmed that owing to these differences the first caliph of the Mirzā had declared that "their Islam (i.e., the Islam of Muslims) is different from our Islam."[204]

In the entire history of Islam, there is one movement alone which appears to bear some resemblance to Qadianism in the sense that while it kept its activities confined to Muslims, it attempted to found a system of beliefs and practices parallel to that of Islam, and thus endeavoured to build, as if it were, a' state within the state. This was the Batinite or Ismailite movement with which Qadianism bears a striking resemblance.[205]

The Qadiani movement tries to build a new structure of religious beliefs and practices as distinguished from that of Islam. It tries to give an orientation of its own to all aspects of religious life. It provides its followers with a new prophet, a new focus of devotion and loyalty, a new religious mission, a new spiritual centre, and a new set of holy places, new religious rituals, new leaders, and new heroes. It is this feature of Qadianism which marks it out from all other schools and sects which exist side by side within the bosom of Islam and raises it to the level of a full-fledged independent religion. It definitely tends to lay foundations of a new ummah on the basis of new religious teachings, and a new mould of religious life. The result is that for those who enthusiastically choose to join the fold of this movement, the old institutions and personalities which claimed their devotion are replaced by new ones, and thus they develop into an ummah all by themselves, independent of all others and by virtue. of their peculiar connaturality of emotional predilections, outlook, and the resultant veneration for the new

---

[204] Khutba (Sermon) of Friday, al- Fadhl, December 3, 1914.

[205] Set Dr. Zahid Ali Our Ismaili religion and our system.

religious institutions formed around Qadianism. This tendency towards isolation, this trend to distinguish themselves from the Muslims has been a part of Qadianism from the very beginning and has since gone the whole length that the Qadianis have now become want to compare Qādiāni rituals and holy places with Islamic rituals and holy places, declaring the former to be parallel and equal to the latter. The companions of the Holy Prophet, for instance, occupy a central position in the religious system of Islam. The Qādiānīs place the companions of the Mirzā on the same pedestal as the 'companions' of the Holy Prophet. A responsible Qādiānī reflects this trend of thinking in the following words:

"To make a distinction between the two groups, that is, the companions of the Holy Prophet and those of the Mirzā, or to declare either of the two to be superior, on the whole, to the other, is not right. In fact, both these groups are part of a single group: the difference is one of time alone. They had been trained under the earlier Prophet while these got instruction at the time of the later prophetic advent."[206]

In the same manner, they consider the grave of the Mirzā to be similar and comparable to the resting-place of the Holy Prophet. Al-Fadhl, published on behalf of the Training Department of Qādiān, once deplored the religious insensitivity of those who came to Qādiān to participate in the religious conference, etc. and yet did not pay a visit to the grave of the Mirzā:

"What is the state of the man who comes to Qādiān, the Abode of Security (*Darul-Amān*), and does not bother to go a couple of steps further to pay a visit to the Heavenly Cemetery: in it is that

---

[206] Al- Fadhl, May 28, 1918.

purified grave (*Rawdha-i-mutahharah*)[207] wherein lies buried the body of that chosen one of God to whom the most superior of all prophets sent his salāms, and with regard to whom the Khatim al-Nabin said: "He will be buried beside me in my grave." Thus, the radiance of the Green Dome of Medina is reflecting itself on this White Dome where one can partake of the blessings which are peculiar to the radiant resting-place of the Holy Prophet (upon him be the peace and blessings of Allah). How unfortunate is the man who, in the Great Pilgrimage (*Hajj-i-Akbar*) of Ahmadism, should remain deprived of this blessing".[208]

Owing to the religious and spiritual importance of the township of Qadiān in Qādiānism, being the nursery of a new prophethood and the new centre of 'Islam', the Qadianis reckon it among the holy places of Islam, such as Mecca and Medina, and never fail to mention it along with them. In one of his speeches, Mirzā Bashiriddin Mahmood said:

"By venerating Medina, we do not affront the House of Kabah. In the same way, when we venerate Qādian, we do not affront Mecca or Medina...... The Exalted God sanctified all these three places and chose them for the manifestation of His Light."[209]

Mirza Ghulam Ahmad had himself drawn a parallel between Qâdiān and the Holy Land of Mecca. In one of his couplets, he said:

[207] It is significant that the same term is generally used by the Urdu speaking Muslims for the grave of the Holy Prophet.

[208] Al- Fadhl, Vol. X No. 48.

[209] Al- Fadhl, September 3, 1935.

The land of Qadian is now a place of veneration. Thanks to the rush of people, it is now a sacred area.[210]

The Mirzā even thought that Qadiān has been referred to in the Qur'an itself, that the 'far-away Mosque' (Al-Masjid al-Aqsa) mentioned in the Qur'an (XVII. 1) refers to the 'Mosque of the Promised Messiah' in Qadian. He wrote:

"In the same way as God had taken the Holy Prophet specially from the sanctified Mosque (in Mecca) to Jerusalem, so He also shifted him temporally from the time of the Glory of Islam, the time of the Prophet himself, to the time of the blessings of Islam, the time of the Promised Messiah. Hence from this point of view, which is the spiritual transportation of the Holy Prophet to the extremity of the time of Islam, the far-away Mosque (al-Masjid al-Aqsā) means the mosque of the Promised Messiah which is located in Qādiān and in respect of which, in *Barahin-i-Ahmadiyah*, God has said: "Blessed, blessed and every blessed thing We shall make therein." And this word 'mubarak (blessed), which has been used nominatively, is in accord with the Quranic verse 'And We blessed that which is around it.' Therefore, there is not the least doubt that there is reference to Qādiān in the Qur'an."[211]

The logical consequence of these beliefs was that the followers of the Mirzā developed the practice of making annual pilgrimage to Qadian, and they began to regard this act as sacredotal as the Hajj itself. It is no surprise that the Qādiāni leaders proclaimed visits to Qādian to be a "shadow of the Hajj", and, for those who are

---

[210] *Durr- i- Thamin*, p. 52.

[211] *Tazkirah or Mujmu'ah- i- Wahy- i- Muqaddas*, pp. 345-46.

incapable of going to Mecca, they proclaimed it to be its substitute. Mirzā Bashıruddin Mahmood said:

"Those alone who have resources and are rich can go on pilgrimages. Although in the beginning divine movements spread and flourished among the poor, only those who have resources and are rich are able to go on pilgrimage. The poor are exempted by the Shariah. Therefore, God fixed a Zilli Hajj so that those whom He wants to employ in the progress of Islam, and the poor, that is, the Muslims of India, should be able to participate in it."[212]

In this regard, the Qādiānīs went so far as to rate these visits to Qādiān even higher than the pilgrimages to the Mecca. This, too, was a natural corollary of their belief in Qādiānism as a new religion which has its own centre of gravity and has undertaken to provide religious sustenance to its followers. It is for this reason that a Qādiānı leader observed:

"In the same way as the former Islam without Ahmadism, that is, without Hazrat Mirzā Sahib, is a dry Islam, so is the Meccan Hajj a dry Hajj without this Hajj, because in these days the objectives of Hajj are not fulfilled there."[213]

This trend among the Qadiānis to assert their distinct entity and their consciousness of being the followers of a new religion, and their feeling that Qadianism had opened a new phase in history, reached such a point that they even introduced a new calendar of their own, which has special names of the months. The twelve months of the Qadiani calendar, according to its official organ, al-

---

[212] Al- Fadhl, December 1, 1932.

[213] *Paygham-i-Sulk*, Vol, XXI, No. 22.

Fadhl, are as given here: *Sulh, Tabligh, Aman, Shahadat, Hijrat, Ihsan, Wafa, Zuhur, Tabuk, Ikha, Nubuwat, Fath.*

Indian Islam

Thanks to this isolationist trend and the belief in a new prophethood, the spiritual, intellectual, and political centre of the Qadiānis soon ceased to be the Arabian Peninsula with its holy cities of Mecca and Medina. Then loyalties began to turn instead towards Qadian, the birthplace of the new religion. It was natural that the Qadianis should became increasingly cool towards Arabia. Hence, those Indian nationalists who felt that the idea of the one nationhood of India was threatened by the fact that a great part of the Indian population was deeply attached to a foreign country, and its religious centre, its spiritual personalities, its holy places and its most cherished memories of history all lay outside the boundaries of India, felt greatly relieved insofar as Qadianism was a purely Indian movement and its spiritual centre lay not outside, but within India. This appeared to them as a very salutary development: a factor which could help the development of a common nationhood in the country.

This orientation of Qadianism was for obvious reasons, welcomed with great zest by those nationalists of India who have always complained that Hijaz has been the real centre of the loyalty of Muslims and that they are always wont to look towards Arabia. To such people this movement appeared as a new ray of hope. A Hindu writer, Dr. Shanker Das Mehra, has very ably represented this standpoint. He has clearly grasped the change in outlook that results from embracing Qadianism. He has also realised the fact that instead of being an Islamic sect, the Qadianis believe in an independent religion and constitute a separate religious community, and that they are engaged in propagating a new religion and building a new community. Dr. Mehra writes:

"The most important question that confronts the country is in what way can national feeling be inspired among the Indian Muslims. At times, pacts and agreements are concluded with them, at times we bargain with them, and, at times, attempt is made to persuade them to unite. But nothing proves of any avail. The Indian Muslims have come to consider themselves a separate nation and they keep on singing praises of Arabia, day in and day out. Had they the power, they would christen India as Arabia. In this darkness, in this state of despair, the Indian nationalists and patriots see only one glimmer of hope. That glimmer of hope is the movement of Ahmadis. The more Muslims will be attracted towards Ahmadism, the more they will begin to consider Qadiān to be their Mecca and will become, in the end, lovers of India and true nationalists.

"The progress of Ahmadism among Muslims can alone deal a deathblow to the Arabic culture and Pan-Islamism. Let us study the Ahmadi movement from the national point of view. From the land of Punjab there arises a man, Mirza Ghulam Ahmad Qadianı, and summons the Muslims:

"O Muslims! I am the prophet whom God has promised to send in the Qur'an. Come! Gather under my banner. If you don't come, God will not forgive you on the day of judgement and you will abide in hell.

"Without entering into any discussion about the truth or falsehood of this claim of the Mirzā, I would like to point out the change that takes place when a Muslim becomes a Mirzāı. A Mirzat Mustim holds it as his creed that:

(1) From time-to-time God sends someone to guide people. Such a person is the prophet of his time.

(2) During the time when moral confusion prevailed in Arabia, God sent Hazrat Muhammad (peace and blessings of God be on him) as His Prophet to that country.

(3) God felt the need of a prophet again, and so He sent the Mirză in order that he should guide the Muslims.

"My nationalist brethren will ask: What have these beliefs to do with nationalism? The reply is that when a Hindu becomes a Muslim, his loyalty and devotion are transferred to the land of Arabia; similarly, when a Muslim becomes an Ahmadi, his angle of vision changes. His devotion to Hazrat Muhammad (peace and blessings of Allah be on him) begins to decrease. Besides, if his caliphate had been in the past in Arabia and the land of the Turks, now it comes to Qādian. Mecca and Medina then remain holy places for him merely in a traditional sense.

"An Ahmadi, whether he is in Arabia, Turkistan, Iran or in any corner of the world, turns towards Qadian for spiritual salvation. The land of Qadiān is the land of salvation for him and therein lies the secret of the superiority of India.

"Every Ahmadi will have love for India, for Qadian is in India. The Mirza too was an Indian, and his Caliphs, who are leading this sect till now, are all Indians."

He adds:

"This is the one reason why Muslims look at the Ahmadi movement with suspicion. They know that Ahmadism is hostile to Arabic culture and Islam. In the Khilafat movement, too, Ahmadis did not join hands with Muslims. For, instead of Turkey or Arabia, they want to. establish the Khilafat at Qadian. This fact, no matter how disappointing to the common Muslims who are always dreaming of Pan-Islamism and Pan-Arab solidarity, is a matter of great joy for a nationalist."[214]

---

[214] Dr. Shankar Das Mehra's article in Bande Matram, April 22, 1932, (cited in Qadiani Mazhab, by Prof. Ilyas Barni).

2: Revolt against Muhammad's Prophethood

The belief that religion has now been perfected, that Muhammad (peace be on him) is the last messenger of God, and that Islam is the last message of God to mankind and the most perfect way of life, is a Divine gift and an honour conferred exclusively on this ummah. It is for this reason that a Jewish scholar had said to Hazrat Umar (may God be pleased with him) that there was a verse in the Qur'an which the Muslims recite. Had that verse been found in the Jewish Scripture, they would have regarded the day of its revelation as a day of national rejoicing and celebration. This Jewish scholar was referring to the Quranic verse which proclaims the termination of prophethood and the perfection of Divine benediction:

"This day have I perfected your religion for you, completed My Favour upon you, and have chosen for you Islam as your religion." (v. 4)

'Umar did not dispute the majestic glory of this Divine proclamation. He only said that the Muslims needed no new celebration for the verse had been revealed on a day which is a day of great devotion and congregation in Islam. The day on which this verse had been revealed was the day of two Ids: The Day of Arafah and Friday.

Security Against Intellectual Chaos

This creed has stood as a great barrier against the disintegrating movements which arose from time to time in the wide expanse of the world of Islam. It is this creed which prevented

Islam from becoming a plaything of false pretenders to prophethood and hypocrites. This creed has been like a fortress wherein this ummah took refuge from the inroads of imposters and adventurers who tried to demolish the entire structure of Islam and to replace it by a new structure. It is, again, this very creed which maintained the religious and ideological unity of this ummah to an extent no other prophet's ummah has been able to do in the past. Had this creed not been there, Muslims would have disintegrated into numerous ummahs, each of which would be having a separate centre of spiritual inspiration, a distinct heritage of cultural traditions and history, and a different set of heroes.

Implications of the Termination of Prophethood

The belief that prophethood has been terminated is a matter of great honour and distinction for mankind. This, in effect, proclaims that mankind has reached the age of maturity and attained the capacity to respond to the last message of God. It means that human beings no longer require any fresh revelation, any further heavenly communication. This belief inspires self-confidence. For man knows that religion has assumed its perfect and final form, and man need no longer look backwards; that humanity needs no longer look towards the heavens for fresh revelation; rather, it should now direct its efforts to make good use of the resources created by God. And in trying to fashion its life according to the fundamentals of religion and morality, it has to look now only towards the earth, and towards its own self. This creed directs the vision of man to the future. It provides an incentive for the creative utilization of man's capabilities. It fixes for man the right goal, and points to the direction in which man should proceed for the achievement of that goal. Without this creed, man would be in a state of doubt, diffidence and hesitation. He would always be looking towards the heavens, instead of looking towards the earth. He would always feel uneasy about his future. Every now and then, some pretender would rise to tell him that "the garden of humanity had remained incomplete" and that it was his advent which had given it its full bloom; leaving man to remain diffident that if it had remained imperfect so far, what was the guarantee for the future! Thus, instead of striving to water that garden, he would always remain waiting for some gardener to come out from above and do the needful.

Qadiani Insolence

Among the different anti-Islamic movements which have arisen in our history, Qadianism is unique. For, if other movements had been directed against Islam as a whole, Qâdiānism is a conspiracy which is specifically directed against the prophethood of Muhammad (peace be on him), and challenges the finality of Islam and the unity of Muslims. By repudiating the finality of prophethood, Qadiānism obliterated the very borderlines which distinguish this ummah from all others. Dr. Sir Muhammad Iqbal has clearly brought out the innovation impudently set afloat by Qādiānism.

"Islam is essentially a religious order which has defined limits, that is, belief in the Unity and Omnipotence of God, faith in the prophets and termination of prophethood on the advent of His last Messenger, Muhammad (peace be upon him). Faith in the last-mentioned creed is, in reality, the distinguishing feature between a Muslim and a non-Muslim and a determinant whether a certain individual or group forms part of the Muslim community or not.

Take, for example, Brahmo Samāj which has faith in God and acknowledges Muhammad as a Prophet of God, but its votaries cannot be treated as Muslims, for, like the Qādiānis, they believe in the continuance of revelation and do not regard the Prophet of Islam as the Last Prophet. As far as I am aware, no sect of Islam has ever tried to go beyond this line of demarcation. In Iran, the Bahäites denied this essential creed, but they also confessed that they constituted a distinct religious order and were not a sect of the Muslims. We believe that Islam, as a religion, has been revealed by God; but Islam as a social order owes its existence to the person of the Blessed Prophet. The Qadiants have, in my opinion, only two ways open to them. They should either follow the Bahāites or accept the creed in regard to finality of Muhammad's prophethood in toto, with its full implications, and give up those far-fetched interpretations which are designed to let them remain within the fold of Islam with a view to enjoying political benefits."[215]

In another article on the subject, Sir Muhammad Iqbal wrote:

"Muslims are unusually sensitive in regard to those movements which pose a danger to their unity. Therefore, every religious group which deems itself historically associated with Islam but has its bases in a new prophethood and treats every Muslim not having faith in its revelations as a non-believer, would be regarded by the Muslims as a danger to the unity of Islam. This is because the sense of Islamic unity springs from the belief in the finality of Muhammad's prophethood."

He adds in the same article that:

---

[215] Iqbal: Harf- i- Iqbal, pp. 136-37.

"It is obvious that Islam, which claims to unite its different sects on the basis of a uniform creed for all, cannot show any sympathy to a movement which presently endangers its own solidarity and is fraught with the danger of further dissension to humanity in future."[216]

Proliferation of Prophets

The natural outcome of the Mirza's preaching against the idea of the finality of prophethood was that the halo of sanctity and veneration, honour and dignity around the office of prophet- hood was gone. The eloquence he waxed on stressing that the process of prophethood had not stopped, the importance he attached to "inspiration", enhancing it to be considered the basis of prophethood, was bound to reduce prophethood to a child's play, even though his argument supporting the continuity of prophethood was confined merely to his own case and he considered himself to be the last prophet. To borrow the remarks of Iqbal:

"The founder's own argument, quite worthy of a medieval theologian, is that the spirituality of the Holy Prophet of Islam must be regarded as imperfect, if it is not creative of another prophet. He claims his own prophethood to be evidence of the prophet-rearing power of the spirituality of the Holy Prophet of Islam. But if you further ask him whether the spirituality of Muhammad is capable of rearing more prophets than one, his answer is "No". This virtually amounts to saying, "Muhammad is not the last Prophet, I am the last." Far from understanding the cultural value of the Islamic idea of finality in the history of mankind generally and of Asia especially, he thinks that finality, in the sense that no follower of Muhammad

[216] Ibid., pp. 122-23.

can ever reach the status of Prophethood, is a mark of imperfection in Muhammad's Prophethood. As I read the psychology of his mind, he seems to be interested only in his own claim to Prophethood; for he avails himself of what he describes as the creative spirituality of the Holy Prophet of Islam but, at the same time, limits this spiritual creative capacity to the rearing of only one prophet, i.e., the founder of the Ahmadiyya movement. In this way the new prophet quietly steals away the finality of one whom he claims to be his spiritual progenitor.[217]

What eludes the grasp of people of normal intelligence is the confinement of Muhammad's prophet-rearing spirituality to one person alone, and that it should have produced no results during the last thirteen hundred years before the advent of the Mirzā nor is it capable of producing any other prophet in the future till the end of time. It is this logic of things which has made Mirzā Bashiruddin Mahmood to make the following observation.

"The Exalted God says about the unbelievers that they did not form a true estimate of Allah and have come to think that the treasures of God have become exhausted, and hence He could not now give anything to anybody. In the same way, (such people) say that no matter how much a man advances in righteousness and piety, and even if he goes ahead of several prophets in divine gnosis and spirituality, God will never, never make him a prophet. This concept is owing to a mis-estimation of God, otherwise, I say that not one, but thousands of prophets will be born.[218]

This trend of denying the finality of prophethood emboldened several people to lay claim to prophethood. So far as we know about

---

[217] Speeches and Writings of Iqbal, pp. 150-51.

[218] *Anwar- i- Khilafat*, p. 62.

the history of Muslim India, there had been none except Akbar who has had the cheek to deny the finality of prophethood and try to promote a new religion. However, even Akbar had not done all that with the outspokenness and vehemence of the Qadianis. The door of prophethood flung open by the Mirzā attracted many an adventurer and pretender. In 1355/1936 Professor Ilyas Barni mentioned seven such pretenders. However, were one to undertake a thorough census of the pretenders in the province of Punjab alone even their number would be much more than seven. This sudden proliferation of 'prophets' caused concern even to the Qadianis, and Mirzā Bashiruddin Mahmood remarked:

"Look at the number of claimants to prophethood who have arisen from the ranks of our own party. Of these, but for one, I believe that none of these is consciously lying. The fact is that in the beginning they received inspirations, and it would be no surprise if they receive them even now. But the mishap was that they erred in the interpretation of their inspirations. I personally know some of these people, and I can testify that they possessed sincerity and fear of God. The Exalted God alone knows how far this opinion is correct, but in the beginning, they were sincere. A part of their inspirations was from God, but the mistake was that they did not grasp the wisdom of the inspirations and foundered."[219]

Dissension Among Muslims

The very idea of the extent to which Muslims will become divided among themselves, and the tragic disintegration that will follow as a result of the rise of these new prophets, makes a Muslim tremble with fear. Secular trends of thought have made people

[219] Al- Fadhl, January 1, 1935.

disinclined to make claims of divinity and prophethood. What would happen, however, if the writings of Mirzā Ghulam Ahmad and the preachings of his followers awaken this idea and there is a proliferation of 'prophets' all over the Muslim world; and each 'prophet' begins to denounce all those who do not come under his banner as Kāfirs. What a colossal intellectual and religious chaos would follow? The world of Islam would become divided into different hostile religious camps and who knows if Muslims too will not experience the religious wars which devastated Europe a few centuries ago. Thus, the ummah which had been raised in order to weld the whole of humanity into one fraternity would itself become a house divided against itself. This danger was realized by one of the followers of the Mirzā, Maulavi Muhammad Ali. Muhammad Ali did not realise, however, that the door to this danger had been opened by his leader, the Mirzā himself. For, in the history of Islam the Mirzā is the only person who initiated a full-fledged movement to prove the unceasing continuity of prophethood. Anyhow, the views of Muhammad Ali are noteworthy:

"Reflect, for the sake of God, that if the belief of Miān Sahib[220] is accepted that the prophets will continue to come and that thousands of prophets will come, as he has written explicitly in *Anwar-i-Khilafat*, will not these thousands of groups denounce one another as Kāfir? And so, what will happen to Islamic unity? Let us assume that all those prophets will be confined to the Ahmadi group alone. Then, how many factions will there be in the Ahmadi group? After all you are aware of what happened in the past, how one of these groups became favourable to and another opposed to the

---

[220] That is, Mirzā Bashiruddin Mahmood. In fairness, however, it should be noted that Mahmood was not the proponent of this idea; he merely reiterated the views of his leader and father, Mirza Ghulam Ahmad.

Prophet after his advent. Then, will that very God who has expressed the will to unify all the peoples of the world at the hands of Muhammad (peace and blessings of God be on him), will He now divide Muslims into numerous factions, each one of them calling the other Kafir, having no Islamic relationship and unity among themselves. Remember that if the promise to make Islam predominant over all religions in the future is true, then that tragic day when thousands of prophets will go about with their own separate factions, when there will be thousands of separate exclusive mosques, each with its own group of mentors of true belief and salvation, denouncing all other Muslims as infidels, will never dawn in the history of Islam.[221]

A Dangerous Hypothesis

A hypothesis of the Mirza, which causes unrest in a Muslim's mind and opens the door of chaos and anarchy in Muslim society is his view that "Divine revelations and communications" are essential for the validity of a religion and a natural outcome of obedience to God and earnest endeavour in His way. In his view, the religion in which "Divine revelations and communications" do not continue unceasingly is a dead and false religion; rather, it is a Satanic religion which leads towards the hell. If the followers of a religion who apply themselves to the practice of austerities and devotion remain deprived of the honour of Divine illumination despite hard efforts and sacrifices in the way of God, they are misguided, unfortunate, and blind. In *Barahin-i-Ahmadiyah* (Vol. V), he wrote:

"What honour, what position, what influence and what Divine strength does that prophet possess, whose followers are merely

[221] *Rädd- i- Takfir- i- Ahl- i- Qiblah*, pp. 49-50.

blind, sightless people, whose eyes have not been opened by Divine communication? How stupid and false is it to believe that after the Holy Prophet (peace and blessing of Allah be on him), the door of Divine revelation has been closed for ever; and in the future, till the Day of Judgement, there is no hope of it being opened again. Keep on worshipping mere fables and stories! Can such a religion, in which there is no direct relationship with God, be a religion in the real sense of the term. What then remains in such a religion except paying devotion to mere fables. Even if a person were to sacrifice his life in His way, even if he were to lose himself completely in striving to gratify Him and prefer Him to everything, even then He does not open the door of His knowledge and does not honour him with communication! I swear in the name of Exalted God that there would be none in this age who would be more averse to such a religion than I. I call such a religion Satanic and not a Divine one and believe that such a religion leads to hell."[222]

Logical Consequences

Assuming "Divine communication" as essential for knowledge and salvation and holding it up as the criterion for the truth and veracity of a religion, the Mirzā turned religion into a highly complicated and an immensely straitened affair, even though God had made it simple and practicable. God says: "God intends every facility for you. He does not want to put you to difficulties."

(II. 185)

"And has imposed no difficulties on you in religion."

(XXII. 78)

---

[222] *Brāhin- i- Ahmadiyah*, Vol. V, p. 183.

"On no soul doth God place a burden greater than it can bear." (II. 286).

But if Divine communication is essential for knowledge and salvation there can be nothing more difficult than religion. For, by nature, an overwhelming majority of people are not disposed to that kind of communication. No matter how hard they try, the door of Divine communication will always remain closed for them. Then, there are those who do have a natural predilection for this, and others there are who do not have the leisure or the Divine help to undertake the vigorous striving essential for such a spiritual achievement. The universal religion which has been designed for the salvation of the whole of mankind and summons all towards God cannot possibly impose such impossible conditions for obtaining the knowledge of God, His propinquity and blessings, and salvation.

If one were to study the Holy Qur'an from one end to the other, one could never find direct communication from God mentioned as an attribute of the believers or of those who merit salvation. Instead, one finds verses which mention characteristics such as those given in the following verses:

"The Believers must (eventually) win through those who humble themselves in their prayers)," (XXIII: 1-2).

"And the servants of the Merciful (God) are those who walk on the earth in humility." (xxv: 63).

Or one might even turn the first page of the Qur'an to find these verses:

"*Alif, Lam, Mim.* This is the Book; in it is guidance, sure, without doubt, to those who fear God; who believe in the Unseen, are steadfast in prayer, and spend out of what We have provided for them:" (II, 1-3).

Nowhere does one find Divine communication mentioned in the Qur'an as essential for being rightly guided or for achieving salvation. On the contrary, the stress is primarily on faith in the Unseen. And faith in the Unseen means a man's acceptance of facts relating to supra-physical matters which cannot be grasped by reason or senses alone, an acceptance based on faith in God's prophet (who had been chosen by God for His revelations). Now, if one were to accept the Mirza's view that Divine communication is essential for true knowledge and salvation, the need for faith in the Unseen becomes superfluous, and the persistent Quranic stress on it difficult to comprehend.

Furthermore, we have before us the lives of the illustrious companions of the Holy Prophet. One might ask: how many of them were honoured by Divine communication? How many can be proved by history or Hadith (Traditions) to have enjoyed that privilege? Nobody who knows the history of those times and understands the temperaments and the circumstances of those people - in fact, no one who grasps human psychology and human nature can say that these companions of the Prophet of God-and their number exceeds the figure of one hundred thousand-had enjoyed Divine communication. When such is the case in respect of the companions, what can be said of those who came after them?

Repudiation of Prophethood

The concept of Divine communication as mentioned above was, in fact, a hidden conspiracy, a clandestine revolt against prophethood as such. If this process were to be considered a widespread one and one of unceasing continuity, prophets would no longer remain necessary at all. The Qur'an and other scriptures link true guidance, knowledge of God, of His Attributes, of His will and all matters relating to the Unseen world, with prophethood. The Qur'an mentions, in the words of the truly-guided believers:

"Praise be to God who hath guided us to this (felicity) Never could we have found guidance, had it not been for the guidance of God. Indeed, it was the truth that the Apostles of our Lord brought unto us." (VII: 43)

At another place, while refuting polytheistic and pagan notions, God says:

"Glory to thy Lord, The Lord of Honour and Power; (He is free) from what they ascribe (to Him). And peace be on the Apostles. And Praise be to God, the Lord, and Cherisher of the Worlds!" (xxxvii: 180:82)

The Qur'an also explains the purpose of the advent of prophets as follows: --

"That mankind after (the coming of) the Apostles, should have no plea against God." (iv: 165)

If one were to examine carefully the concepts preached by the Mirzā regarding the continuity of Divine communication and takes note of his view that it was essential for one's salvation, it would reveal not only a spirit of revolt against the finality of prophethood but would reveal symptoms against the very idea of prophethood. In fact, if these concepts were to be taken seriously, religious faith would become something akin to the spiritual feats such as occultism, which are becoming popular in the present times.

Source of Divine communication

Then, what is the criterion of these communications? And what is the guarantee that these communications did not reflect either the inner being of the person himself, or his environment, or his peculiar upbringing, or his sub-conscious desires, or else the complex of factors related to his heredity? Those who have studied the ancient collections of these communications know that the bulk of them consists of completely erroneous hypotheses and concepts which had their origin in ancient mythology. Look at the spiritual experiences and Divine communications of the Neo-Platonists of Egypt. Were they not merely geared to the support of the idolatrous mythology and philosophical hypotheses of the time? Even during the Islamic period some of the people who had a deep faith in things such as Divine communication and craved for gnosis mention having met Aristotle and having talked to him, which reflects the peculiar mental outlook of ancient philosophy, or Greek mythology. And if one studies the Divine communications which the Mirza claims to have received one finds in them incontrovertible reflections of the time and environment of his life, his upbringing, his subconscious urges; on the whole, a reflection of the degenerate and decadent society in which he had been reared and wherein he preached his message. In fact, these communications contain far enough evidence to force anyone who knows the political history of modern India to the conclusion that the real source of the Mirza's inspiration was the political authority ruling over the country. Iqbal, who was a man of rare insight and had also studied the Qadiani movement thoroughly, has made the following observation:

"I dare say the founder of the Ahmadiyya movement did hear a voice, but whether the voice came from the God of Life and Power or arose out of the spiritual impoverishment of the people must depend upon the nature of the movement which it has created and the kind of thought and emotion which it has given to those who have listened to it. The reader must not think that I am using metaphorical language. The life-history of nations shows that when the tide of a people begins to ebb, decadence itself becomes a source of inspiration; inspiring poets, philosophers, saints, and statesmen and turning them into a class of apostles whose sole ministry is to glorify, by the force for a seductive art or logic, all that is ignoble and ugly in the life of their people. These apostles unconsciously clothe despair in the glaring garments of hope, undermine the traditional values of conduct and thus destroy the spiritual virility of those who happen to be their victims. One can only imagine the rotten state of a people's will who are, on the basis of Divine authority, made to accept their political environment as final. Thus, the actors who participated in the drama of Ahmadism were, I think, only innocent instruments in the hands of decadence."[223]

[223] Iqbal Speeches and Writings, pp. 157-58.

3: The Lahori Branch

The branch of Qadianism which has had its headquarters until recently at Qadian and was later transferred to Rabwah under the second Khalifah and the Mirza's own son, Bashiruddin Mahmood, has made the Mirza's prophethood its fundamental article of faith. With great frankness and courage this group adheres to this belief. No matter how objectionable this creed might be from the Islamic viewpoint, this group deserves the credit for having adopted a clear and categorical standpoint and showing moral courage. It is also beyond doubt that this group faithfully represents the teachings of the Mirzā, in so far as he had claimed prophethood for himself in clear and vigorous terms.

But the standpoint of the Lahore branch, whose leader until a few years ago was Maulavi Mohammad Ali (d.1952), is enigmatic to the core. Anyone who has studied the writings of the Mirzā knows that he explicitly claims prophethood and regards all those who disbelieve in his prophethood to be Kafirs. If the meanings of words are fixed, and they have to be taken in the sense in which the speakers of that language understand them, and if Mirzā had written his books in order to convey his message to his compatriots, then there can be no doubt that he did say that he was a prophet, that he had received revelation, that he was entitled to prescribe divine ordinances and injunctions, that he was the bearer of shariah (Divine Law), and that the one who rejected him was a Kafir and doomed to hell-fire. But Maulavi Muhammad Ali seems to have had greater sympathy with the Mirza than he had for himself or his offsprings have for him. It appears that Maulavi Muhammad Ali is keen to protect the greatness of the Mirzā and his religious services and perhaps is trying, both consciously as well as sub-consciously, to keep his own deep attachment to, and veneration of, the Mirzā intact and, at the same time, to spare his soul and his religious conscience the torment caused by the Mirzā's shocking claim to be a prophet and the consequent ex-communication of the Muslims, who rejected him, as Kāfirs. Muhammad 'Alī tries to show that the Mirzā never claimed prophethood in the technical sense of the word. Wherever the Mirzā used terms like prophethood (nabüwah) revelation (Wahı) and disbelief (Kufr), in Muhammad Ali's opinion he used them in a mystical (Sufis) sense, that is, these words have an allegorical and metaphorical import. It is obvious that if well-known and commonly used religious terms were to be taken as sufistic mysteries, or as allegories and metaphors, then the writings and statements of any person can be interpreted in all possible ways and no connotation can be fixed for any piece of writing.

Maulavi Muhammad Ali considers the Mirzā to be the greatest Mujaddid and reformer of the fourteenth century (of Hijrah), and above all that, the Promised Messiah. It is at this point that the two branches of Qadianism meet. Even in his commentary of the Holy Qur'an, there are indications that he considered the Mirzā to be the Promised Messiah. For instance, at one place in his Urdu commentary of the Holy Qur'an he writes:

"Muhammad (peace and blessings of God be on him) was sent to all mankind and his time extends to the Day of Judgement. And, hence, to consider oneself to be in need of some other messenger or prophet is ingratitude to this great benefactor. Thus, the prophecy about the advent of the son of Mary in the Hadith can only mean that someone of this ummah will come bearing resemblance to the son of Mary. This corresponds to the prophecy of the second advent of Elijah (Ilyas) which was fulfilled by the coming of John (Yahyā) in the manner of Elijah. This statement of the Noble Qur'an prevents Jesus from coming back personally to the Muhammadan ummah."[224]

In his works, too, he generally refers to Mirzā as "the Promised Messiah[225]. However, here we would confine ourselves to a glance at his commentary of the Holy Qur'an in order to find out his religious attitudes and tendencies.

A study of his commentary of the Holy Qur'an shows that Muhammad Ali's mind had almost completely assimilated Sir Sayyid Ahmad Khan's mode of thinking as well as his method of interpreting the Qur'an. His close contact with Hakim Nūruddin and his lessons in exegesis (Tafsir) of the Qur'an from the latter further reinforced the tendencies he had imbibed from Sir Sayyid Ahmad Khan. In fact, Mohammad Ali is a typical example of the kind of people found among the Muslims today. He is keen to present the Qur'an before the modern world and before those educated in the modern tradition. At the same time, his own mental framework and his intellectual upbringing prevent him from accepting facts relating to the Unseen World and the facts not comprehended by limited human intellect. He represents, therefore, the attitudes of those Muslims who have accepted all the results of modern scientific research, or to be more accurate, they have accepted the well-known concepts of science-as distinguished from scientific facts-as axiomatic and have set them up as the criterion for the acceptance or rejection of everything, including the teachings of religion and the contents of heavenly scriptures. Such people have a frame of mind which is, on the whole averse to belief in the Unseen World

---

[224] *Tafsir Bayan al- Qur'an*, Vol. I, p. 317.

[225] See for example, his *al- Nabiwah fi al- Islam* and also *Radd- i- Takfir* of the people of the Qiblah.

and in miracles. At the same time, they also have a religious inclination which makes them disinclined to repudiate the clear texts of the Qur'an. Hence, they try to strike a middle path. They interpret the Quranic texts relating to the Unseen World and miracles in such a manner as would not go counter to the concepts and ideas in vogue in the present times. In short, it is an attempt to make Islam palatable to the modern mind. To achieve this end, Muhammad Ali interprets Quranic verses in a highly arbitrary and exotic manner. He goes to a ridiculous length of casuistry in order to support his interpretation on the basis of the feeblest of evidence. In these explanations he sets aside all that might stand in the way of making Qur'an conform to the whims and inclinations of the modern man. The accepted principles of Tafsir, the rules of language and literature, the known usages of terms, the understanding of these terms on the part of the companions of the Prophet and Arabic-speaking people, the exegesis of the earlier scholars, all these are rejected out of hand to show that Quranic verses have nothing which can be regarded as 'out of fashion' in the present age. In this his comments are very similar to those of Sir Sayyid Ahmad Khān. Below are a few examples which will show Muhammad 'Alī's adventures in the realm of Quranic exegesis:

(1) In the Second Chapter of Qur'an, it has been said that when Moses (peace of God be on him) prayed to God (for water for his people in a wilderness), he was asked to strike with his staff. This made twelve springs gush forth, and the twelve tribes of the Israelites drank to their full. The Quranic verses read:

"And when Moses prayed for water for his people, we said: Strike the rock with thy staff. So there flowed from it twelve springs. Each tribe knew its drinking place." (iv: 60)

If one were to interpret this verse in the light of the words in which this incident has been conveyed and in the way it has been understood by all since the day it was revealed to the Prophet, one would be forced to the conclusion that this was a supernatural event brought about in a manner contrary to the natural law of causation. However, such an occurrence is, obviously, contrary to normal human experience and runs counter to our understanding of physical and geological laws. This forced Muhammad Ali to interpret it in quite a novel way. Let us reproduce what he has to say on the point:

"The words *idrib biasa ka-l-hajara* may be translated in two ways, strike the rock with thy staff, or march on or go forth or hasten, to the rock with thy staff. Darb means striking, smiting, marching on, going from place to place, setting forth a parable, and carries a number of other significances. In fact, *darb* is used to indicate all kinds of actions except a few (*Taj al-Arus*). When *arda* (land or earth) is its object, it carries the significance of going about or seeking a way. Thus *daraba-l-ard* or *darab fi-l-ardhi*, both signify he journeyed in the land or went forth or hastened in the land (Arabic-English Lexicon by Lane). The object of *idrib* here is *al-hajar,* which means a rock or a mountain to which there is no access. Asa ordinarily means staff or rod, but its primary significance is a state of combination (*Taj al-Arus* and Lane's Lexicon), and the word is metaphorically used to speak of a community. Thus, of the Khawarij, a Muslim sect, it is said *Shaqqa asa-l-Muslimina* (lit. they broke the staff of the Muslims, which means that they made a schism in the state of combination and union, or in the community of the *Muslims-Lisan al-Arab*). Hence, the words may mean strike the rock with thy staff or march on to the mountain with thy staff or thy community. What the words of the Qur'an signify is either that Moses was commanded by God to smite a particular rock with his staff from which water flowed forth miraculously, or to march on to a mountain from which springs flowed."[226]

What is significant about this interpretation of the verse put forth by Muhammad Alı is that the latter alternative has been preferred by him because affirmation of miracles appears old-fashioned and "un-scientific".

(2) Another instance is his explanation of the following verse:

"And when you killed a man, then you disagreed about it. And Allah was to bring forth what you were hiding. So, we said: Smite him with a part of it. Thus, Allah brings the dead to life, and He shows you His signs that you may understand."

(II: 72-73)

Now, the general Muslim interpretation of the incident is that an Israelite had been killed, and the Israelites were not succeeding in tracing out the murderer. The successors of the dead asked Moses to find out from God who the murderer was. Earlier, the Israelites had been asked to slaughter a cow, which they had done after considerable hesitation and with a feeling of remorse. In order to show the wisdom and reward of their compliance with Divine commandment, God ordered them to smite the dead man with some part of slaughtered cow, which would make the dead man tell the name of the murderer. This was a very effective means of teaching the Jews the blessings of honouring and obeying God's commandments. In fact, anyone who goes through these Quranic verses without any preconceived notion is bound to interpret it in

[226] Muhammad Ali's English Commentary, p. 29.

no other manner. But since this involved a categorical affirmation of miracle, Mohammad 'Ali explains the verses quite differently:

"The story generally narrated by the commentators to explain this passage is not based on any saying of the Holy Prophet, nor is it met with in the Bible. The very indefiniteness of the incident is an indication that it refers to some well-known event in history, and as almost all incidents of the stubbornness of the Jewish nation prior to the time of Jesus have been mentioned, it becomes almost certain that this incident refers to Jesus himself, as it was with respect to his death that disagreement took place, and many doubted his death. This inference becomes stronger when we compare the incidents narrated here with the same incidents as narrated in the fourth Chapter vv. 153-57, when after enumerating almost all the incidents narrated here in the three previous sections, the Qur'an goes on to accuse the Jews in the following words "And they are saying: Surely we have killed the Messiah, Jesus, son of Mary, the messenger of Allah and they killed him not. nor did they crucify him, but he was made to appear to them as such, and those who differ therein are surely in doubt about it; they have no knowledge representing, it, but only follow a conjecture" (4: 157). The part quoted answers exactly vv. 72 and 73, only the name is omitted here. The comparison makes it clear that it is the apparent killing of Jesus that is referred to here. The words that you killed (Arabic: gataltum) are used, because in the first place the Jews asserted that they had killed him, and, secondly, because metaphorically a man may be said to have been killed when he is made to appear as if he were dead."[227]

[227] Muhammad Ali's English Commentary. p. 34.

As for the part of the verse which mentions the order to smite the dead body, he explains the phrase "a part of it", as follows:

The construction of the phrase *idritrbuhu bi badi-ha* is rather difficult, but a comparison with 4: 157 makes the meaning clear. Darb.........conveys a number of significations. It means striking as well as likening, and as an instance of the latter significance, we find in the Qur'an itself, where it is said *Yadribu-llahu-l-Haqq wa-l-Batila*, 'Allah compares truth and falsehood." (XIII: 17)

"In *badı-ha* (lit, a part of it) the personal pronoun *ha* i.e. it refers to the act of murder. The act of murder was not completed in the case of Jesus, as the Gospels show, for after he was taken down from the cross his legs were not broken as in the case of the thieves. The meaning of the sentence is therefore according to the signification of *darb* that we adopt: strike him with partial death or liken his condition to that of the partially dead man, and thus he was made to appear as a dead man, as stated in 4:157. There is no other case of murder or an attempted murder in Jewish history of which the whole nation could be said to have been guilty, and which might answer to the description of these two verses.'[228]

This type of reasoning is fairly illustrative of the mentality we have spoken of above. In order to avoid affirming a miracle all kinds of involved reasoning is employed, including the contention (see the above citation) that the feminine pronoun was used as masculine, and the incident of Jesus (peace be on him) was tagged on to these verses, without there being for it any contextual relevance whatsoever.

---

[228] Ibid. p. 35

(3) The Qur'an repeatedly mentions that to provide evidence of his prophethood, Jesus made from clay the form of a bird, and then he breathed into the model, which sprang into life and flew into the air like a real bird.

"And I made for you from clay the form of a bird, then I breathe into it, and it came a bird with Allah's permission."

(II:49)

The verse obviously suggests a miracle. In order to avoid that, Muhammad 'Alī gives an out-and-out figurative interpretation of the verse. His interpretation of the verse is novel since he assigns an altogether novel signification to the four terms used in the verse: *Khalq*, *tin*, *nafkh*, and *tair*. *khalq* according to him, here means the determining of a thing. As for tin and *nafkh*, he says, "Man is spoken of as being created from tin or dust, which stands for his humble origin, but the *nafkh* or breathing into him makes him deserve of respect by the angels." Then comes the word *tair* which, says Muhammad 'Alī, means a bird just as the word *asad* (lit, a lion) is figuratively used for a brave man. In a parable, it is quite unobjectionable, says Muhammad Alī, to take the word (air as signifying one who soars into the higher spiritual regions and is not bent low upon earth or earthy things. In the light of these novel significations given to the words, Muhammad Ali considers the verse to mean:

"So that is meant here is that Jesus, by breathing a spirit into mortals, will make them rise above those who are bent upon the earth, and the apostles of Jesus, who were all men of humble origin (which is referred to in the word dust in the parable), whose thoughts had never risen higher than their own humble cares, left everything for the master's sake and went into the world by the command of the master, preaching truth. Here was, no doubt, mere dust having the form of a bird, which the messenger of God converted into high-soaring birds by breathing the truth into them."[229]

(4) The Qur'an mentions Solomon enumerating the favours of God unto him. He said:

"On man, we have been taught the speech of birds, and we have been granted of all things." (xxvii: 16).

Since knowledge of "speech of birds" is contrary to normal human experience, Muhammad Ali considers the knowledge of speech of birds to mean Solomon's use of birds for conveying messages. In his own words:

"Solomon's understanding of the speech of birds may imply that he made use of birds to convey messages from one place to another, these messages being metaphorically called the speech of birds."[230]

The following verse reads:

"Till when they came to the valley of the ants, the she-ant said: "O ants, enter your abodes." (xxvii: 18).

Here again, Muhammad Ali gives a free rein to his imagination. According to him, Wad al-Naml does not mean, as it apparently does and as it has been interpreted by exegetists, the 'valley of ants', but the valley of an Arab tribe called Banu Namlah,

---

229 Muhammad Ali's English Commentary, p. 144.

230 Ibid.

and the word namlah (she-ant) mentioned in the verse has been explained by him as follows:

"It is the name of a tribe......The name Namlah used also to be given to a child in whose hand an ant was placed at its birth, because it was said that such a child would be wise and intelligent."[231]

(5) In the Quranic chapter entitled Saba it has been mentioned about Solomon:

"But when We decreed death for him, naught showed them (the *jinn*) his death except a creature of the earth who ate away his staff." (XXXIV: 14)

The Muslim exegetists in explaining this verse point out that Solomon was having his temple constructed by jinn. When he came to know that the time of his death had arrived, he explained the plan of construction to the jinn, shut himself up in a house of glass, and devoted himself to the worship of God. In this state, the angel took the breath of life out of him. His corpse kept standing by the support of a wooden staff. The jinn kept on working for long. None sensed that Solomon had died. When the construction was completed, the staff which had supported his corpse fell down because of its having been eaten up by a moth. It was then that his death became known. The jinn also realised the limitations of their knowledge of the Unseen. Their human followers too came to realise that had the jinn become aware of Solomon's death by virtue of their capacity to know the Unseen, they would have got rid of the humiliation they had been enduring so long.

---

[231] Ibid., p. 731.

Now, since all this could be accepted only if supernormal things are affirmed, Muhammad 'Alī again comes forward with a strange explanation. This is what he has to say on the question:

"The reference in the creature of the earth that ate away his staff is to his son's weak rule, under whom the kingdom of Solomon went to pieces. It appears that Solomon's successor, Rehoboam, led a life of luxury and case, and instead of acting on the advice of older men, he yielded to the pleasure-seeking wishes of his companions (Kings: 12:13), and it is to his luxurious habits and easy mode of life that the Holy Qur'an refers when it calls him a creature of the earth. The eating away of his staff signifies the disruption of the Kingdom. The jinn, as already remarked, mean the rebellious tribes who had been reduced to subjection by Solomon, and who remained in subjection to the Israelites for a time. until the Kingdom was shattered."[232]

(6) Another example of the same trend is his explanation of the following verse:

"And he reviewed the birds, then said: How is it I see not hudhud or is it that he is one of the absentees." (27:20)

The word *hudhud* has been understood as signifying a particular species of birds (hoopoe). The same view is corroborated by the context because a little earlier there is a mention of Solomon's knowledge of the speech of birds, and, again, since it is the birds that he is reviewing. But since it is not normal that a human being should converse with birds and call it to account, and the bird should explain its conduct before him, Muhammad Ali let

---

[232] Muhammad Alis English Commentary. p. 825.

his imagination loose and interpreted *hudhud* as the chief officer of Solomon's Department of Intelligence. He wrote:

"By *Hudhud* is not to be understood lapwing, but a person of that name. In many languages, many of the proper names given to men will be found to be identical with the names of animals. The Arab writers speak of a king of Himyar as Hudad (Lisan al-Arab), which is almost identical with Hudhud mentioned in the Qur'an...... The verses that follow show clearly that Solomon was speaking of one of his own officers.

In his Urdu Tafsir, he elaborates the situation, pointing out that Hudhud was an intelligence officer and that when Solomon reviewed the birds who were used to carry on intelligence work, he found the officer of the intelligence department, Hudhud, absent. (See his Tafsir al-Bayan, VOL. III, P. 1413)

(7) The Qur'ân mentions the existence of a distinct species called Jinn, inter alia, in the following verse:

"Say: It has been revealed to me that a party of the jinn listened, so they said: Surely we have heard a wonderful Qur'ân." (LXXII:1)

The testimonies of Qur'an and Hadith, the continuity of Muslim belief, as well as human observations, are too overwhelming on the question to warrant the denial of the existence of a separate species of ethereal beings. Muhammad All too could not explicitly reject this belief as erroneous. He merely seems to evade the question. He tries, therefore, to give other meanings of the term, depending upon the contexts in which the term occurs. At one place, he considers the word jinn to signify "great potentates or powerful leaders who, through their importance and detachment from the masses, do not mix freely with them, so they remain distant or "hidden" from their eyes."[233] No less strange is his feat imagination in trying to explain that the term in the Quranic verse mentioned above refers to Christians.[234] He regards the opening verses of this chapter as prophetical, "speaking of some future time when Christian nations forming the bulk of mankind-such being one of the significances of the word jinn (Lane's Lexicon)-will accept the truth of the message brought by the Prophet."[235]

These are just a few examples. The huge Commentary of Muhammad Ali is replete with such distortions under the immature impression that modern science was opposed to belief in miracles or in the occurrence of an event which is of a supernatural order.

At this point a sound thinking person is bound to ask himself the question: did the Companions of the Holy Prophet, who were the first addressees of the Qur'an, and in whose mother-tongue the Qur'an was revealed and who had the honour of having been instructed by the Holy Prophet himself, also understood the same import of the verses as has been explained by this new- fangled exegetist? Did they also think that 'strike the staff on the rock' meant 'march on to the mountain with thy community? Did they also think that 'And strike him with part of it' means 'kill him only partially'? Did they also think that the claim of Jesus of 'creating birds out of clay' meant 'infusing the spirit to rise above earthly concerns? Did they also think that 'the speech of birds' meant 'message-carrying birds', that the 'creature of the earth' referred to Solomon's son, Rehoboam, and that 'jinn' meant the 'Christian

---

233 Muhammad Ali's English Commentary, p. 306.

234 Ibid., p. 1107.

235 Ibid., p. 1107.

nations of Europe'? In the same way, did any of the followers of these companions, or any Arab linguists, or scholars and exegetists understand something similar to what Muhammad Ali understood from them? It would be hard to say 'Yes' for we have before us the entire treasure of Tafsir literature and it testifies to the originality of Mohammad "Ali's brain. None of the profound scholars of Arabic and its literature can even imagine that these verses could, by any stretch of imagination, mean what this non-Arab scholar thinks they mean, almost for the first time after more than thirteen hundred years.

This being the case, one is left wondering about the significance of the Quranic claim of being a 'clear book' which has been revealed in 'clear Arabic.' The Qur'an itself makes the claim in these words:

"And surely this is a revelation from the Lord of the Worlds. The faithful spirit has brought it on thy heart so that thou mayst be a Warner in plain Arabic language." (XXVI: 192-95)

"These are the verses of the Book that makes manifest. Surely we have revealed it - an Arabic Qur'an-that you may understand." (XII: 1-2).

Another verse says:

"And certainly, We have made the Qur'an easy to understand. Now, is there anyone who will ponder"? (LIV: 17)

If Muhammad Ali's approach were to be considered sound, it would mean that for more than thirteen hundred years the Qur'an remained an incomprehensible mystery, an unsolved puzzle. To disregard the obvious meaning of Quranic verses, to set aside the well-known rules of Arabic language and grammar, to neglect the interpretations of Qur'an made by the companions of the Prophet, to overlook the context of relevant Prophetic Traditions-all this means subjecting the Qur'an to distortion and reducing it to a plaything. This is a great danger and portends ill for Muslims if people promoting this kind of approach find an encouraging response from them. Long ago Mirza Ghulam Ahmad made a very apt remark about the Tafsir of Sir Sayyid Ahmad Khān. Nothing could apply more adequately to the Tafsir of Muhammad Alt. He said:

"These interpretations of the Holy Qur'an, which were neither in the knowledge of God's Prophet, nor in the knowledge of his companions, nor in the knowledge of saints and *aqtab* and *ghāwth* and *abdal*, nor have any direct or indirect textual evidence, have caught the imagination of Sir Sayyid."

4: Contribution of Qadianism to the Muslim World

Now that we have studied the life of the founder of Qādiānism, traced the evolution of its doctrines, and noted its doctrinal emphasis, etc., we are in a position to attempt historical evaluation of Qadiānism and see what achievements go to its credit in the history of the reformist movements in Islam? What has it given to the present generation of Muslims? What has been the practical outcome of this religious hullabaloo, which has been going on for about three quarters of a century? The founder of the movement has bequeathed a whole library of his works on all kinds of religious subjects, particularly controversial matters, and they have been under discussion for over seventy years. What is the essence of these works, and what are they really driving at? What is the message of Qadianism for the present age?

To answer these questions, we should cast a glance at the Muslim world itself, wherein this movement arose. We should also have a look at the state of the Muslim world during the second half of the nineteenth century, and its problems and difficulties.

The most important event which took place during this period of time, which can be ignored neither by a historian nor a reformer is the aggression of Europe on the Muslim world, particularly India. The educational system that came in its train was devoid of the spirit of god-consciousness, and the culture which sprang from this new world-view was permeated with ungodliness and sensuality. The world of Islam fell an easy prey to this nascent but militarily well-equipped European power because it had become impoverished in all respects: in respect of faith, of knowledge, and of material resources. This was the time when a conflict of colossal importance took place: the conflict between religion (and Islam alone was in the field to represent religion) and the ungodly and materialistic culture of Europe. This conflict gave birth to a large number of political, cultural, intellectual and social problems-problems which could have been solved only through strong and unshakeable faith, profound and extensive knowledge and extraordinary self- confidence and perseverance. To encounter this situation, the Muslim world needed a great spiritual and intellectual personality who could infuse the spirit of jihad (struggle) in the Muslim world, unite the Muslims, be able to withstand the least distortion of Islamic teachings, bring about a rapprochement between the eternal message of Islam and the restless spirit of the present age by dint of his strength of faith and intellectual acumen, and meet squarely the challenge of the zestful and buoyant West.

This was one aspect of the problems faced by the Muslim world of that time. The other aspect of the Muslim world was that it appeared to be infested with religious and moral ailments, the most gruesome of which was the rise of doctrines and practices which bore the imprint of polytheistic influences. Tāziās and graves were worshipped. People swore in the names of others than God. Innovations in religion were popular everywhere. Superstitions and meaningless beliefs were rampant. This situation called for a reformer of tremendous dimensions: a reformer who could purge the Islamic society of anti-Islamic influences, remind the Muslims of the true doctrine of Tawhid, and stress the obligation of adhering to the Sunnah of the Prophet; in short, one who could thoroughly purify the religious life of Muslims.

Besides this, the contact with foreign nations and a materialistic culture had begun to corrode, the Muslims socially and degenerate them morally. Moral degeneration had gone to the extent of unabashed sinfulness; love of extravagant and luxurious living to the extent of licentious self-indulgence; docile obedience to their rulers to the extent of intellectual subservience and loss of self-respect; and, the tendency to imitate the Western culture and the way of life of their British masters to the extent of the repudiation of the teachings of Islam. The situation obviously demanded the rise of a great crusader against these degenerating tendencies, a crusader who would put a stop to the tidal waves of moral and intellectual decline and counteract the harmful effects of political slavery and its offshoot of mental bondage.

Again, there was the problem of ignorance: the ignorance of even the rudiments of Islam on the part of a great majority of Muslims. As for the people educated along modern lines, they were unaware of Islam, of the normative principles of the Muslim way of life, of the history of Islam, and of the greatness of their own past, and were, on the whole, pessimistic about its future. Islamic religious sciences were in a state of decay, and the old centres of learning appeared to be on the verge of collapse. All this meant that a new, vigorous educational movement was needed, a movement to set up new schools and madrassās, as well as to produce forceful books in order to improve the knowledge of Muslims about their religion, awaken their religious consciousness and create in them a deep faith in the teachings of Islam.

Even more important than all these was another crying need of the Muslim world: the need to summon the Muslims in the manner of the prophets, to live a truly Islamic life characterised by strong faith and righteous action. It is this alone which entitles the Muslims to the help of God, to their predominance over the enemies, and to their salvation in this world as well as in the next and every kind of felicity and honour. The fact is that the real need of the

Muslim world has never been, nor will it ever be a fresh religion: all that it has needed is a fresh and deeper faith in Islam. Never has the world of Islam needed a new religion, or a new prophet. It has merely been in need of a fresh faith in, and fresh enthusiasm for, the eternal truths: the beliefs and the teachings revealed to the last of all the prophets, Muhammad (peace be on him). This faith is adequate enough to encounter the evil tendencies that might arise in any age and resist the new temptations that the changing time brings along with it.

In response to the crying needs of the Muslim world mentioned by us, there arose numerous personalities and movements in the Muslim world. They made no big claims, nor did they try to create a new ummah. All they did was to fulfil these important needs as best as they could, and in so doing, they inspired a great number of Muslims. They neither tried to promote a new religion, nor invited people to rally around some new prophet, nor did they create anarchy in Muslim ranks. They wasted none of their capabilities in futile tasks. Such personalities and movements proved to be an unmixed blessing to the Muslim world, their mission was free from all possibilities of harm, and their work, commendable beyond any shadow of doubt. Without having lost anything, the Muslims benefited from them and to them they owe a heavy debt of gratitude.

At such a critical movement, in the most crucial area of the Muslim world, India, which was the main scene of intellectual and political conflicts, there also arose Mirza Ghulam Ahmad to initiate a new movement. What is noteworthy about him is that he totally disregarded some of the most important problems which were confronting the Muslim world in his days and focused all his attention on one question alone. Now, what was it? The question of the death of Messiah and the claim on his own part to be the Promised Messiah. Whatever time and energy was left after concentrating on this issue was spent on propagating that jihad had become prohibited and that loyalty to the British Government was a religious imperative. For about a quarter of a century these very questions continued to be debated by him at great length. If the writings of the Mirza on the question of Messiah were to be expunged from his works, hardly anything of significance will be left in them.

Moreover, it is also to be noted that the Mirzā raised the standard of his prophethood and declared all those who did not accept his claim as kafirs in a Muslim world which was already torn by dissensions. By so doing, however, the Mirzā raised an iron wall between himself and the Muslims. On the one side of this wall there are a few thousand followers of the Mirzā, and on the other side is the rest of the Muslim world which stretches from Morocco to China and has great personalities, virtuous movements of reform, and valuable institutions. They stand isolated from and opposed to the whole of this world. Thus, he unnecessarily added to the difficulties of Muslims, further aggravated their disunity and added a new complication to the problems facing them.

The Mirzā has made no worthwhile contribution to the intellectual and religious heritage of Muslims, which would call for his recognition and because of which he might deserve the gratitude of the present generation of Muslims. Nor did he initiate a broad-based movement for the revival of Islam which could profit the Muslims as a whole, nor help Muslims to solve any of the major problems facing them, nor did his movement contain any message for the contemporary civilization which is in the grips of a major crisis and is interlocked in a life and death struggle. Nor can he even be credited with any significant achievement vis-à-vis the expansion of Islam either in India or Europe. His message remained addressed to the Muslims and of necessity could only lead to mental confusion and unnecessary religious squabbles within the Muslim community. If the Mirzā can be considered successful, it is only in so far as he bequeathed to his family the legacy of spiritual leadership and worldly prosperity, the legacy of a kind of theocracy in which respect he is comparable to the Agha Khan and his ancestors.

The fact is that it is merely a set of favourable circumstances and not any inner vitality which accounts for the survival of Qadianism for several decades. It owes a good deal to the intellectual bewilderment found in India, and particularly in Punjab in his time. Qadianism is also indebted to the dominance of the British in India, which had weakened the bases of Islamic life so that the rising generation of Muslims had become profoundly ignorant of the teachings of Islam and the characteristics and attributes of prophethood and true spiritual leader- ship. It owes a debt of gratitude to the encouragement and patronage it received from the British rulers. Had it not been for these factors, Qadianism which bases itself mainly on inspirations, dreams, fantastic interpretations of religious texts and dry and lifeless theological quibbling, which have no moral and spiritual message for the present age, nor any imaginative solution for the problems of our time, could never have remained alive as long as it has managed to do in this degenerate and confused generation. It seems to me that we have been punished by God for the ingratitude that Muslims have shown to Him in the past by deviating from the teachings of Islam, and the crimes we have committed by not fully recognizing the true servants of the cause of Islam who rose amidst us. For all these crimes we have received what we unfortunately deserved this intellectual plague and the rising up of this man amidst us, who has sown the seeds of perpetual discord and disunity.

A few years ago, while lecturing at the University of Damascus on the movements of reform and revival of true Islam in the past, I made the following observation about the Batinite movement, which appears worth reproducing in the context of Qadianism:

"When I read the histories of Batinite movement, of Ikhawan al-Safa, of Bahāism in Iran and Qadianism in India, it seems to me that when the founders of these movements read the history of Islam and the life of the Prophet it struck them that a man, all by himself stood up with a mission in Arabia, without any money to back him, or any army to support him; he summoned people towards a creed, towards a religion and not after very long there came into existence a new ummah, a new state, and a new culture. They also noticed that single-handed he changed the direction of human history and forced events to flow into a different channel. The ambitious natures of these men then whispered to them: "Why not try?" These people knew that they had intelligence, remarkable mental capabilities and organising ability. They thought, therefore, that history might repeat itself in their case, following the natural pattern of cause and effect. These people had expected the same kind of miraculous success to crown their efforts, as had crowned the efforts of the unlettered Prophet of Arabia in the sixth century, for, they thought that human nature remained always the same, and if it had responded to Muhammad in the past, there was no reason why it should not respond to them now.

"These persons did have a glimpse of the greatness of Muhammad (peace be on him), who carried his movement to a successful end, but could not see. the Divine support which was his real strength, nor the Divine Will of which he was an instrument.

"The result was that for a very short period of time, the efforts of these ambitious people did bear some fruit. There gathered behind them a following, sometimes of several hundred thousand people. Some of them (e.g. Bātinites) even succeeded in establishing a state of their own (the Fatimide State) which for some time covered a fairly wide area from Sudan to Morocco. But all this remained only as long as they were able to maintain their organisation- al efficiency, their wizardry and their secret administrative network. But when these things were gone, all their power and glory also became a poignant memory of the past. With the loss of worldly power, the religious movement shrank and obscured and lost all significance for human life. Against this, is the true Islam preached by the last messenger of Allah (peace be on him). It constitutes today, as it constituted yesterday: a great spiritual force in the world, the guiding star and inspiration of a great ummah. It still possesses a distinctive culture which sprang from the spirit of its teachings. It is still the religion of a number of states and peoples, The sun of Muhammad's prophethood is still shining brilliantly in the sky. Never in history has it suffered an eclipse and it never will."

Bibliography

Mirza Ghulam Ahmad Qadiani: Al- Arbain, Vols. I- IV, II Edition (1920)

Ajaz- i- Ahmadī (1902)

Aina- i- Kamalat- i- Islam, Ahmadiyah Anjuman Isha'ät- i-Islam, Lahore (1893)

Aik Ghaltı As Izālah

Al- Wasiyat

Anjam- i- Atham (1897)

Asmanı Faislah, Zia- al- Islām Press, Qadian (1917)

Izāla-i-Awhām, III Edition (1902)

Barahin- i- Ahmadiya, Vols. I- V, IV Edition (1884 and 1907)

Fath-i-Islam (1891)

Haqiqat- al- Wahi

Khutbat- i- Ilhamiyah

Kitab- al- Bariyah, II Edition (1932)

Najm al- Huda

Nazul- al- Masih

Nur- al- Haqq

Shahna- i- Haq Vol. I

Sitārah Qaisariyah

Surma-i-Chashm-i-Arya, I Edition, Gulzar-i-Hind Press, Lahore (1886)

Shahadat- al- Qur'an, Sher Hind Press, Amritsar

Tiryaq- al- Qulüb, Zia- al- Islam Press, Qådiān

Tazkirah or Majmu'à Wahi Muqaddas

Tawdih- al- Maram

Tuhfat- al- Nadwa, Zia- al- Islam Press, Qādian

Mirza Bashiruddin Mahmood: *Anwar- i- Khilafat;*

Aina- i- Sadaqat

Barkat- i- Khilafat

Durr- i- Thamin

Haqiqat-an-Nabiwah; A Present to His Royal Highness the Prince of Wales (dated January 19, 1922)

Mirza Bashir Ahmad: Sirat- al- Mahdi, Vols. I and II, II Edition (1935)

Kalamatul Fast

Muhammad 'Ali: *Bayan- al- Qur'an*, Karimi Press (1941) Commentary of the Holy Qur'an (English version of the Tafsir Bayan- al- Quran) *An Namwah fil Istam Radd- i-Takfir- i- Ahl- i- Qiblah;*

Haqiqat- i- Ikhtalaf Mir Qasim Ali Qadiani: *Tabligh- i- Risalat*, Vol, VI, VII, x

Sheikh Yakub 'Ali 'Irfanı (ed.): *Hayat- i- Nasir; Maktubat- i- Ahmadiyah*, Vol. V

Akbar Shāh Khān Najibābādı: *Mirqat- al- Yaqın in Hayat- i- Nüruddin, Anjuman Isha'at- i- Islam* Ahmadiyah Buildings, Lahore

S. Sarwar Shāh Qādiānī: *Kashf- al- Ikhtalaf, Zia- al- Islām* Press, Qādian, (1920)

Qazi Fazal Ahmad: *Kalama- i- Fazl- i- Rahmani*

Anwar Shah: *Aqidat- al- Islam*

Sir Syed Ahmad Khan: *Asbab Baghawat- i- Hind*

Dr. Abdul Haq: Chand Ham Asr

Dr. Abdul Hakim: *Az- Zikr- il- Hakim*

Rahat Malik: Daur Hazir ka Mazhabı Aamir

Dr. Zahid Ali Our smart religion and its system

Dr. Sir Muhammad Iqbal: Pas Che Bayad Kard; *Zarb- i- Kalim: Harf- i- Iqbal*

Writings and Speeches

Prof. Salahuddin Flyās Barni: Qadiani Madhab, Umdatul Matābe, Lucknow

Ibn Hazam: *Al- Fast fi Milal* and Nahl

Ibn Hajar: *Fath- ul- Bari*

Maulana Abdul Hai: *Nuzhatul Khawatir*, Vol. VI, *Da'iratul Ma'arif*, Hyderabad

Sir William Hunter: Our Indian Mussalmans

Daily Papers and Journals

The Daily *Paigham-i-Sulh*, Lahore, Vol. XXI, No. 22

Journal *Tashkhiz- i- Azhān*, Qādian, Vol. VI, No. 14; Vol. IX, No. 11

The Daily Al-Hukm, Qadiān: Issues of August 10, 1901, April 14, 1908, May 7 and 21, 1934

Journal 'Review of Religions', Qadian, Vol. VII, No. 726 of June-July, 1908 Vol. XIV, No. 6

Journal *Mi'ar- ul- Ikhbar*

Journal *Ishaat-i-Sunnah*, Amritsar, Vol. VII, No. 6 of June, 1884

The Daily Al-Fazl, Qadian, Issues of December 31, 1914,

May 28, 1918, December 15, 1921, December 18, 1922, January 4, 1923, March 3, 1925,

August 6, 1925, April 13, 1926, April 29, 1927, July 3, 1931, February 23, 1932, December 1, 1932, January 1 and 15, 1935, September 3, 1935 and September 15,1936.

www.ingramcontent.com/pod-product-compliance
Ingram Content Group UK Ltd.
Pitfield, Milton Keynes, MK11 3LW, UK
UKHW021406190726
13845UKWH00028B/916

9 789394 770577